From
Amish and
Mennonite
Kitchens

As a tradition, Amish and Mennonite cooking feeds the soul as well as the body. Richly nutritious, this food can quickly become a celebration. Here are choice from-scratch recipes, newly tested and tasted, set forth in easily followed steps. The resulting dishes are sturdy and basic, yet full of flavor, affection, and warm memories of big kitchens.

From Amish and Mennonite Kitchens

Phyllis Pellman Good *and*
Rachel Thomas Pellman

Good Books

Intercourse, PA 17534

from
Amish and Mennonite
kitchens

Cover artwork and design by Cheryl Benner.
Design by Craig Heisey.
Calligraphy by Gayle Sollenberger Smoker.

FROM AMISH AND MENNONITE KITCHENS
Copyright © 1984, 1998 by Good Books, Intercourse, PA 17534
International Standard Book Number: 0-934672-21-0
Library of Congress Catalog Card Number: 84-80653

Library of Congress Cataloging in Publication Data
Good, Phyllis Pellman,
   From Amish and Mennonite kitchens.

   Includes index.
      1. Cookery, Amish. 2. Cookery, Mennonites. I. Pellman,
Rachel T. (Rachel Thomas) II. Title. III. Title: Amish and
Mennonite kitchens.
TX715.G61725 1984   641.59748   84-80653
ISBN: 0-934672-21-0

Contents

from
Amish and Mennonite
kitchens

Table Prayer

Enable us to use Thy manifold blessings
  with moderation;
Grant our hearts wisdom to avoid excess
  in eating and drinking
  and in the cares of this life;
Teach us to put our trust in Thee
  and to await Thy helping hand.

—Traditional Amish Prayer

Introduction --

As a tradition, Pennsylvania Dutch cooking feeds the body as well as the soul. Richly nutritious, this food can quickly become a celebration.

Amish and Mennonite cooks most often work from scratch. They have at hand the basics, and their tutors have been their own mothers and grandmothers. So they draw upon the fruits of the farm and the "feel" and experience only a seasoned cook can teach.

Two characteristics of these people's lives have shaped their eating: traditionally, they have worked hard physically, and they have chosen a disciplined life. Because of their intense labor, they have eaten heartily and heavily. And, although restrained in their choice of clothing, home decor, and use of money, and little entertainment, they have celebrated extravagantly around food.

Many Pennsylvania Dutch mothers show their affection more easily with a cherry crumb pie or hamloaf rather than with hugs and kisses. Food, in this setting, belongs to some of the warmest human

from
Amish and Mennonite
kitchens

experiences—family reunions, going to Grandma's, making ice cream on a summer evening, getting together to can and freeze.

Young Amish and Mennonite cooks face a new challange—how to maintain the love and celebration this food offers, while eliminating some of its calories that were less troublesome in a more physically active time. But together these cooks are refining the old dishes for today. This food has always sustained physical life while nurturing community life. There's no reason to believe that should change now!

Here, then, are the old favorites, newly tested and tasted for everyone's use.

~Phyllis Good and Rachel Pellman, Editors

About the Amish and Mennonites --

The Amish and Mennonites are much like an extended family. With many branches, each with its own particularities, the groups are still more alike than different.

They all have common faith rooting. Their beginning can be traced to the time of the Protestant Reformation in sixteenth-century Europe. In 1525 a group of believers parted company with the established state church for a variety of reasons. Among them was the conviction that one must voluntarily become a follower of Christ, and that that deliberate decision will be reflected in all of one's life.

Eventually the group was called Mennonites after Menno Simons, one of their leaders. Over the years these people grew into a strong faith community, concerned with the nurture and discipline of each other.

Basic to their beliefs was a conviction that if one was a faithful follower of Christ's, one's behavior would clearly

from
Amish and Mennonite
kitchens

distinguish one from the larger world. These people saw themselves as separated unto God because of their values of love, forgiveness and peace. Because they were misunderstood and because they appeared to be a threat to the established church and government, the people were often persecuted and many became refugees.

In 1693, a charismatic young Mennonite leader believed that the church was losing some of its purity and that it was beginning to compromise with the world. So he and a group who agreed with him left the Mennonites and formed a separate fellowship. They were called Amish, after their leader, Jacob Amman. Today the Amish identify themselves as the most conservative group of Mennonites.

In general, the Amish tend to be more wary of interchange with the larger world than Mennonites are. They are more distinctly separate in lifestyle. The Old Order Amish do not own or drive cars, they live without electricity, have prescribed dress patterns, operate their own schools, and speak Pennsylvania Dutch among themselves, a language which further defines their group. They are also cautious about doing missions.

In general, the Mennonites have been more open to give-and-take with the larger world, accepting technology and education, being less distinctively different in lifestyle, and being active in mission work. They have fostered group identity by working at making church central to social life and Christian faith the motivation for one's training or choice of job or how one uses money.

But none of these are static people. Nor are these generalizations categorically true. There are Amish groups who use technology and promote higher learning. And there are Mennonites who drive horses and buggies, follow nonconformity in their dress and prefer farm-related occupations.

Food is not a part of the religion of any of these people. But their bountiful meals, their tenderly-preserved fruits, and their rich baking are all part of the very fabric of their lives. They have respectfully cultivated the land—and it has returned to them abundant gardens and thriving livestock.

Breads

from
Amish and Mennonite
kitchens

Breads

A warm, moist, pungent smell through the house. A steaming loaf of bread just lifted from the oven. It's breadbaking day!

Once a weekly chore, bread is baked less frequently these days. But the old choice recipes are easily dusted off on a cold winter day or for a special holiday meal.

Thoughts of cinnamon rolls, glazed doughnuts, and corn pone will make any child hungry for home. For these foods are rich in flavor and affection and warm memories of big kitchens full of love.

Breadbaking is a practiced art. Procedures aren't usually written down; instead they're learned at mothers' and grandmothers' elbows. So we asked some experienced bakers to explain their methods. Then our testers tried them and refined them for everyone's use. These are traditional recipes. And delectable!

Breads

Bran Muffins

Makes 12 muffins

1 cup bran
½ cup whole wheat flour
½ cup wheat germ
½ cup sunflower seeds (optional)
1 cup raisins
3 tsp. baking powder
1 egg, well beaten
1 cup milk
⅓ cup oil
2 Tbsp. molasses
1 tsp. vanilla

1. Combine all dry ingredients. In separate bowl, combine all wet ingredients.
2. Pour wet ingredients over dry ingredients, mixing only till moistened.
3. Fill muffin pan about ¾ full. Bake at 350° for 20 minutes.

"They're healthy — and the kids love them!"

from
Amish and Mennonite
kitchens

White Bread

1 pkg. dry yeast	Makes 2 loaves

½ cup warm water
⅓ cup sugar
2 tsp. salt
2 cups warm water
2½ Tbsp. melted shortening
6-7 cups flour

1. Dissolve yeast in ½ cup warm water.
2. In large bowl combine sugar, salt, water, and shortening. Add yeast mixture. Gradually add flour to form a soft dough. Turn onto floured surface and knead until smooth. Place in greased bowl. Cover and let rise about 2 hours. Punch down. Divide into 2 portions and form loaves. Place in greased bread pans. Prick tops with fork. Let rise until higher than pans (about 2 hours).
3. Bake at 375° for 25-30 minutes. Cool 10 minutes. Butter tops of loaves. Place pans on sides until loosened. Remove bread and cool completely.

Whole Wheat Bread

2 pkgs dry yeast   Makes 4 loaves
4 cups warm water
½ cup soft margarine or butter
¼ cup molasses
½ cup honey
2 tsp. salt
6 cups whole wheat flour
4 cups white flour

1. Dissolve yeast in warm water.
2. Combine margarine, molasses, honey, and salt. Mix well. Add yeast mixture. Gradually add flour. Turn onto floured surface and knead until smooth. Place in greased bowl and let rise until double. Punch down. Let dough rest a few minutes. Shape into 4 loaves. Place in greased bread pans. Let rise about 1 hour. Bake at 375° for 35-40 minutes.

Said the tester, "This is the best loaf of brown bread I ever made!"

Breads

Potato Bread

Makes 3 loaves

3½ cups milk
6 Tbsp. sugar
6 Tbsp. butter
2 tsp. salt
½ cup mashed potatoes
2 pkgs. dry yeast
½ cup lukewarm water
3 cups whole wheat flour
7-8 cups white flour

1. Scald milk. Add sugar, butter, salt, and mashed potatoes. Cool to lukewarm.
2. Meanwhile, dissolve yeast in water. Add to cooled milk mixture.
3 Add whole wheat flour and 1 cup white flour. Beat 2 minutes with mixer. Stir in 6-7 more cups flour until dough leaves sides of bowl.
4. Turn onto lightly floured surface. Knead lightly till dough forms a smooth ball. Place in greased bowl. Turn once to grease top of dough. Cover and let rise in a warm place away from drafts until doubled, 1½ - 2 hours. Punch down and let rise again till double. Turn onto floured surface and divide dough into 3 equal parts. Cover

and let rest 10 minutes.
5. Form 3 loaves and place in greased bread pans which have been sprinkled with cornmeal (about 1 Tbsp. per pan.)
6. Bake at 350° for 40-45 minutes. Remove from pans and place on rack to cool.

Steamed Bread Dumplings

Make your favorite white bread dough. When ready to be baked, take part of the dough and form bun size balls. Place in a buttered baking dish (about 2" deep) and steam over boiling water for 30 minutes. Serve hot with fruit and milk.

"These can be served also as dessert with sliced canned peaches and milk."

Oatmeal Bread

Makes 2 loaves

1 pkg. dry yeast
½ cup warm water
1 cup quick oats
½ cup whole wheat flour
½ cup brown sugar or molasses
1 Tbsp. salt
2 Tbsp. margarine
2 cups boiling water
5-6 cups flour

1. Dissolve yeast in warm water.
2. In large bowl combine oats, whole wheat flour, sugar, salt, and margarine. Pour boiling water over all and mix well. When mixture is cooled to lukewarm stir in yeast.
3. Stir in approximately half of flour. Turn onto floured surface and knead in remaining flour.
4. Place in greased bowl. Cover and let rise until double. Punch down. Shape into two loaves and place in greased bread pans. Let rise again. Bake at 350° for 30-40 minutes. Cool on rack, brushing loaves with margarine for a soft crust.

Rye Bread

Makes 3 loaves

1 pkg. dry yeast
½ cup warm water
2 cups rye flour
¾ cup dark molasses
⅓ cup shortening
2 tsp. salt
2 cups boiling water
6-6½ cups white flour

1. Dissolve yeast in warm water.
2. In large bowl, combine rye flour, molasses, shortening, salt, and boiling water. Mix well. Cool to lukewarm. Add yeast mixture. Gradually add white flour to make a soft dough. Turn onto floured surface and knead well.
3. Place dough in greased bowl. Turn once to grease surface. Cover and let rise until double (about 1½-2 hours). Punch down in bowl. Cover and let rise again until double (about 30 minutes). Turn onto floured surface. Shape into 3 loaves and place in well greased bread pans. Let rise again (about 30 minutes). Bake at 350° for 35-40 minutes. Remove from pans. Cover loaves with dish towel and cool on racks.

Ada's Dill Bread

Makes 3 loaves

2 pkgs. dry yeast
1 cup warm water
2 cups warmed cottage cheese
4 Tbsp. sugar
2 Tbsp. minced onion
3 tsp. dill weed
2 tsp. salt
½ tsp. baking soda
2 eggs
1 Tbsp. oil
5½ - 6½ cups flour

1. Dissolve yeast in warm water.
2. Combine all ingredients except flour and beat well. Add flour gradually. Turn onto floured surface and knead until smooth.
3. Place in greased bowl and let rise until double. Punch down. Divide dough into 3 portions and form loaves. Put into 3 greased bread pans and let rise again.
4. Bake at 350° for 30 minutes. Lay foil over top of loaves to prevent over-browning and bake 15 minutes longer.

Raisin Bread

Makes 5 loaves

1 15 oz. box raisins
2 Tbsp. dry yeast
1 cup warm water
2 cups warm milk
½ cup oil
½ cup sugar
1 Tbsp. cinnamon
1 Tbsp. salt
2 eggs, beaten
8-10 cups flour

1. Soak raisins 3-4 hours or overnight. Drain.
2. Dissolve yeast in warm water.
3. Combine milk, oil, sugar, cinnamon, salt, and eggs. Beat well. Add yeast and raisins.
4. Gradually add flour, stirring by hand. When dough becomes too stiff to stir, finish working in flour with hands.
5. Place dough in greased bowl. Cover and let rise in warm place about 1 hour. Punch down, knead and let rise another hour. Divide dough into 5 portions and form loaves. Place in greased pans and let rise another hour.
6. Bake at 300° for 50-60 minutes.

Breads

Sweet Rolls

Makes 2 dozen

1 pkg. dry yeast
¼ cup warm water
¼ cup shortening
¼ cup sugar
1 cup milk, scalded, or 1 cup water
1 tsp. salt
1 egg, beaten
3¼ - 4 cups flour

1. Dissolve yeast in warm water.
2. In large bowl, combine shortening and sugar. Pour hot milk or water over mixture. Cool to lukewarm. Add 1 cup flour and beat well. Beat in yeast mixture and egg.
3. Gradually add remaining flour to form soft dough, beating well.
4. Brush top of dough with softened shortening. Cover and let rise in warm place until double (1½ - 2 hours). Punch down and knead. Form rolls. Let rise again until doubled. Bake according to variation instructions below.

Variations:

1. Divide dough in half. Roll each half into a rectangle approximately 12" x 8". Spread with butter and sprinkle with a

mixture of ½ cup brown sugar and 1 tsp. cinnamon. Roll as a jelly roll. Cut into 1-1½" slices. Place rolls in greased pans about ¾" apart. Let rise and bake at 350° for 30 minutes. Cool and spread with confectioner's sugar icing.

2. For pecan rolls, place ½ cup pecans in bottom of each of two greased 9½ x 5 x 3 inch pans. Make syrup by heating slowly: ½ cup brown sugar, ¼ cup butter, and 1 Tbsp. light corn syrup. Divide this syrup in half and pour half over each pan of pecans. Make rolls as in variation #1, cutting sugar to ¼ cup, and place on top of pecans and syrup. Let rise till double and bake at 375° for about 25 minutes. Remove from oven and turn pan upside down onto a flat plate. Syrup will run down through the rolls and pecans will be on top.

3. Make rolls as in variation #1, but sprinkle with raisins before rolling up. Bake as in #1.

Breads

Orange Rolls

1 cup shortening
⅔ cup sugar
1 Tbsp. salt
2 cups milk, scalded
3 Tbsp. dry yeast
1 cup warm water
½ cup orange juice
4 Tbsp. grated orange rind
4 eggs, beaten
11-13 cups flour

1. In large bowl, combine shortening, sugar, and salt. Scald milk and pour over shortening mixture.
2. Dissolve yeast in warm water.
3. When milk mixture is cooled, add orange juice, rind, eggs, and yeast. Mix well.
4. Gradually add flour, mixing with spoon. After adding about 8 cups, place on floured surface and knead in remaining flour.
5. Place in greased bowl and let rise till double. Roll about ¾" thick and cut with biscuit cutter. Place in greased baking pans about 1 inch apart. Let rise until double.
6. Bake at 325° for 20-25 minutes.
7. When cooled ice with Orange Icing.

Orange Icing

    4 Tbsp. orange juice
    1 Tbsp. grated orange peel
    3 cups 10x sugar

Combine and mix until smooth.

Cinnamon Flop

    1 cup sugar   Makes 2 9" pans
    2 cups flour
    2 tsp. baking powder
    1 Tbsp. melted butter
    1 cup milk
    brown sugar, cinnamon, and butter for top

1. Sift sugar, flour, and baking powder together.
2. Add butter and milk and stir until well blended.
3. Divide mixture between 2 9" pie or cake pans, well greased.
4. Sprinkle tops with flour, then brown sugar, then cinnamon. Push chunks of butter into the dough. This makes holes and later gets gooey as it bakes. Bake at 350° for 30 minutes.

Breads

from
*Amish and Mennonite
kitchens*

Cinnamon Rolls

Makes 4 dozen

½ cup sugar
½ cup shortening
1½ tsp. salt
1 cup milk, scalded
1 cup lukewarm water
2 pkgs. dry yeast
2 eggs, beaten
½ tsp. nutmeg (optional)
7 cups flour

Filling

6 Tbsp. melted butter
1½ cups brown sugar
1 Tbsp. cinnamon
1 cup raisins (optional)

1. In large bowl, combine sugar, shortening, and salt. Scald milk and pour over shortening mixture.
2. Combine yeast and warm water and set aside to dissolve.
3. When milk mixture has cooled, add beaten eggs, dissolved yeast, and nutmeg. Beat well.
4. Gradually add flour, beating well. Turn onto floured surface and knead lightly,

adding only enough flour so dough can be handled. Place in greased bowl. Cover and let rise in warm place until double (about 2 hours).

5. Divide dough in half. Roll each piece into rectangles. about ¼" thick. Brush with melted butter and sprinkle with mixture of brown sugar and cinnamon. Sprinkle with raisins. Roll up like jelly roll and cut slices ½" thick.

6. Place slices 1" apart in greased baking pans. Let rise about 1 hour.

7. Bake at 375° for 20 minutes.

"These always bring ooh's and aah's from guests!"

Breads

from
Amish and Mennonite kitchens

Sara King's Doughnuts

¾ cup lard or shortening   Makes 2½ dozen
¾ cup sugar
1 cup hot water
1 cup warm water
2 pkgs. dry yeast
2 eggs, beaten
1 tsp. salt
6 or more cups flour

1. In large bowl combine shortening, sugar, and warm water.
2. Add yeast to water and set aside to dissolve.
3. When shortening mixture has cooled, add eggs, salt, yeast mixture, and flour.
4. Turn dough onto floured surface and knead until smooth and elastic. Cover and set in warm place. Let rise until double. Roll dough about ½" thick and cut with drinking glass or doughnut cutter without the hole. Let rise again until double.
5. Fry doughnuts in deep fat until browned, turning once. Cool and fill. To fill, cut a small hole with a sharp knife. Force filling into doughnut with a cookie press or cake decorator.

Filling

    4 cups 10x sugar
    1½ cups shortening
    2 egg whites
    2 Tbsp. flour
    2 tsp. vanilla
    4 Tbsp. milk

Combine all ingredients and beat until smooth.

Quick Waffles

    4 eggs   Makes 10-12 waffles
    2½ cups milk
    ¾ cup melted shortening
    3½ cups flour
    6 tsp. baking powder
    1 tsp. salt

1. Combine all ingredients and beat for 1 minute.
2. Bake waffles in hot waffle iron.

Breads

Glazed Potato Doughnuts

Makes 3½ dozen

1 pkg. dry yeast
¼ cup warm water
¼ cup shortening
¼ cup sugar
½ tsp. salt
1 cup scalded milk
¾ cup mashed potatoes
2 eggs, beaten
4-6 cups flour

1. Dissolve yeast in warm water.
2. Combine shortening, sugar, salt, and milk. Cool to lukewarm. Add yeast mixture, potatoes, and eggs. Beat well. Gradually add flour to make a soft dough. Turn onto floured surface and knead well. Place in a greased bowl. Cover and let rise until double (1-1½ hours). Punch down and let rest 10 minutes. Roll dough ½ inch thick. Cut with doughnut cutter. Let rise until double. Deep fry in hot oil (375°). Glaze or sprinkle with powdered or granulated sugar.

Breads

Glaze
  1½ lb. confectioner's sugar
  1½ Tbsp. melted butter
  1½ tsp. vanilla
  warm milk (enough to make a soupy
              consistency)

Dip doughnuts in glaze. Allow excess glaze to drip off.

A drinking glass and a baby bottle may be used as a doughnut cutter. The top of the bottle makes the hole.

A word from the tester: "My two neighbor ladies helped me and responded by eating _most_ of them!"

Potato Doughnuts

Makes 2½ dozen

1 cup mashed potatoes
1½ Tbsp. melted shortening
2 eggs
½ cup milk
¼ cup sugar
½ tsp. salt
⅛ tsp. nutmeg
1 Tbsp. baking powder
2½ cups flour

1. Combine mashed potatoes and shortening. Add eggs and milk and beat well.
2. Gradually add dry ingredients and spices, mixing well.
3. Roll dough ¼ - ½ inch thick. Cut with doughnut cutter and fry in hot fat until nicely browned.

"When it's cold outside, serve these by the fireplace with tea."

Date and Nut Loaf

Makes 1 loaf

1 cup chopped dates
1 cup boiling water
1 tsp. soda
1 cup sugar
1 Tbsp. butter
1 egg
1 cup walnuts
1½ cups flour
1 tsp. vanilla

1. Sprinkle dates with soda and pour boiling water over all. Set aside.
2. Cream sugar, butter, and egg. Gradually stir in walnuts, flour, and vanilla. Combine with date mixture.
3. Pour into ungreased, paper-lined loaf pan or 8½ × 11 inch pan. Bake at 350° for 40-45 minutes.

"We usually serve this in the late afternoon at Christmas family gatherings."

Breads

from
Amish and Mennonite
kitchens

Pumpkin Bread

3 cups sugar
1 cup oil
4 eggs
1 tsp. nutmeg
1 tsp. cinnamon
1½ tsp. salt
2 cups pumpkin, cooked and mashed
⅔ cup water
1 tsp. soda
½ tsp. baking powder
3 cups flour

1. Combine sugar, oil, eggs, nutmeg, cinnamon, and salt. Beat well.
2. Add remaining ingredients and mix well.
3. Pour batter into 2 loaf pans or 3 1-lb. coffee cans, which have been well greased. Bake at 350° for 1 hour. Slide bread out of pans or cans and cool.

Variations:
1. Add 1 cup chopped pecans to batter.
2. Add ⅔ cup raisins to batter.

Homemade Zucchini Bread

Makes 2 loaves

3 eggs
2 cups sugar
2 cups zucchini, shredded
1 cup cooking oil
2 tsp. vanilla
3 cups flour
1 tsp. salt
1 tsp. soda
1 tsp. baking powder
2 tsp. cinnamon
½ tsp. nutmeg
¼ tsp. cloves
½ cup chopped nuts
½ cup raisins (optional)

1. Beat eggs till foamy. Stir in sugar, zucchini, oil, and vanilla.
2. Gradually add dry ingredients and spices. Stir in nuts.
3. Pour into bread pans which have been greased only on the bottoms. Bake at 325° for 60-80 minutes. Cool 10 minutes. Remove from pans and cool completely. May be used as bread or frosted and served as cake.

Breads

from
Amish and Mennonite
kitchens

Old Fashioned Walnut Bread

3 cups sifted flour   Makes 1 loaf
1 cup sugar
4 tsp. baking powder
1½ tsp. salt
1 egg, lightly beaten
¼ cup shortening, melted
1½ cups milk
1 tsp. vanilla
1½ cups walnuts, coarsely chopped

1. Sift together flour, sugar, baking powder, and salt.
2. Combine egg, shortening, milk, and vanilla and add to dry mixture. Stir just until all flour is moistened. Stir in walnuts.
3. Turn into a greased loaf pan or divide between 2 greased 2½ lb. cans. Bake at 350° for 80 minutes for loaf pan or about 70 minutes for cans.

Variation:
1. Blend ⅓ cup brown sugar, 1½ Tbsp. flour, 1 tsp. cinnamon, and 2 Tbsp. butter together. Prepare batter as directed. Pour half into loaf pan. Sprinkle streusel mixture

over batter. Top with remaining batter. Bake according to instructions.

2. Add 2 tsp. grated orange peel to egg and milk mixture. Add ¾ cup chopped candied fruit with the walnuts.

Green Tomato Bread

Makes 2 loaves

3 eggs
1½ cups sugar
1 cup vegetable oil
1 tsp. salt
1 Tbsp. vanilla
2 cups grated, drained, green tomatoes
3 cups flour
1¼ tsp. soda
½ tsp. baking powder
¾ cup raisins
1 cup chopped nuts

1. Beat eggs well. Add sugar, oil, salt, vanilla, and tomatoes.
2. Sift dry ingredients together. Gradually add to tomato mixture. Stir in raisins and nuts.
3. Pour into greased bread pans and bake at 350° for 45 minutes.

from
Amish and Mennonite
kitchens

Corn Pone

1 cup sugar   Fills 1 9"x 13" pan
½ cup butter or shortening
2 eggs
1½ cups cornmeal
1½ cups flour
3 tsp. baking powder
½ tsp. salt
1½ cups milk

1. Cream sugar and shortening. Add eggs and beat well.
2. Combine cornmeal, flour, baking powder, and salt. Add alternately with milk.
3. Pour into a greased and floured 9"x 13" cake pan. Bake at 350° for 45 minutes.

Corn Meal Cakes

½ cup flour   Makes about 20 cakes
1½ cups yellow roasted corn meal
2 tsp. baking powder
1 Tbsp. sugar
1 tsp. salt
1½ cups milk
1 Tbsp. liquid shortening

1. Combine all ingredients. Mix well.
2. Fry on greased griddle or skillet until browned.

Breads

Corn Meal Mush

   1 qt. boiling water   Makes 2½ quarts
   1 qt. cold water
   2 cups yellow roasted corn meal
   ½ cup white flour
   1 tsp. salt

1. Put 1 qt. boiling water in a heavy 4 qt. saucepan. Combine corn meal, flour, and salt and stir into boiling water.
2. Slowly add cold water, stirring constantly to prevent lumps.
3. Cover and cook slowly 1-3 hours just so mixture glops slowly.
4. Serve hot with cherry pie filling or thickened sour cherries and milk.

Note:
   Pour remaining mush in bread pan. Next day, slice and fry in oil for breakfast. Serve with molasses or syrup.

Apple Fritters

Makes 12 fritters

1 cup flour
1½ tsp. baking powder
½ tsp. salt
2 Tbsp. sugar
1 egg, beaten
½ cup plus 1 Tbsp. milk
1½ cups apples, pared and diced

1. Sift dry ingredients together. Beat egg and add milk. Pour into dry ingredients and stir until batter is smooth.
2. Pare and dice apples. Add apples to batter and blend well.
3. Drop by spoonfuls and fry in hot fat in heavy skillet. Fry until golden brown on both sides.

Variation:
    Apples may be cored and sliced in round rings. Dip in batter and fry until golden brown.

Soda Biscuits

Breads

2 cups flour   *Makes 12 biscuits*
1 scant tsp. soda
1 scant tsp. cream of tartar
pinch of salt
3 Tbsp. shortening
1 cup sour milk or buttermilk

1. Rub dry ingredients and shortening together to make fine crumbs.
2. Add milk, stirring with fork until soft dough is formed.
3. Roll ½ inch thick and cut with biscuit cutter.
4. Bake at 450° for 10-12 minutes or until lightly browned.

Serve warm with butter and molasses or with gravy.

"My mother used this recipe a lot."

Soups

from
Amish and Mennonite
kitchens

Soups

A bowl of homemade soup can warm any occasion. Rich yet simple, filling yet not fattening, this is basic, sturdy fare.

Good soup recipes have come about as a result of overabundant gardens and the impulse to never waste a thing. Flavorful broths don't depend on fine meat cuts. Vegetables—whether fresh, frozen, or dried—in almost any imaginable combination cook up into tasty stews.

Soup makes a hearty breakfast, a quick lunch, or a respectable supper (shored up with plenty of sandwiches!). And the range is nearly boundless. We've selected the favorites (complete with rivels), from Old Time Beef Stew to Cold Bread Soup. Aunt Esther's Potato Soup may vary a bit from Grandma Metzler's but the basics are the same. So try your own additions to these—and make them yours!

Corn Chowder

2 slices bacon   Makes 4-6 servings
1/4 cup chopped onion
2 medium potatoes, cubed
2 cups corn
1/2 cup chopped celery
1/2 tsp. salt
1/4 tsp. pepper
2 cups chicken broth
2 Tbsp. flour
2 cups milk

1. In 3-quart saucepan fry bacon until crisp. Remove and drain, reserving drippings. Crumble bacon and set aside.
2. Cook onions in bacon drippings until soft but not brown. Add potatoes, corn, celery, salt, pepper, and 1½ cups chicken broth. Bring to a boil. Reduce heat. Cover and simmer 15-20 minutes.
3. Blend flour and remaing chicken broth. Add to vegetable mixture. Cook and stir until slightly thickened and bubbly. Reduce heat.
4. Add milk. Heat thoroughly but do not boil. Top with crumbled bacon.

Soups

Chicken Corn Rivel Soup

3-4 lb. stewing chicken   Makes 8-10 servings
2 Tbsp. salt
¼ tsp. pepper
1½ cups celery, chopped
1 medium onion, chopped
2 Tbsp. minced parsley
1 quart corn (fresh, frozen, or canned)
Rivels

1. In large kettle cover chicken with water. Add salt and pepper. Cook until soft. Remove bones and skin from chicken and cut meat into small pieces.
2. Heat broth to boiling point and add remaining ingredients. Cook about 15 minutes. Add meat. Heat thoroughly. Garnish with hard-boiled egg or parsley.

Rivels

1 cup flour
1 egg
¼ cup milk

1. Combine flour and egg. Add milk.

Mix rivels by cutting with two forks to make crumbs the size of cherry stones. Drop rivels into boiling broth while stirring to prevent rivels from packing together.

Chicken Rice Soup

Makes 6 servings

1 whole chicken, cut apart
2 quarts water
1 onion, chopped
¾ cup celery, chopped
1½ tsp. salt
dash pepper
1 cup rice, cooked

1. In a large kettle combine chicken, water, onion, celery, salt, and pepper. Cook until chicken is tender, about 1½ hours.
2. Remove chicken from broth and pick meat from bone. Return to broth with rice. Heat thoroughly.

Vegetable Soup

Makes 8 servings

1 beef soup bone
2 quarts water
1 tsp. salt
1 cup carrots, diced
½ cup celery, diced
1 quart tomatoes or tomato juice
1 small onion, chopped
2 quarts mixed vegetables
1½ cups potatoes, diced
1½ cups cabbage, thinly sliced
1 cup macaroni
½ cup rice

1. Cook soup bone with salt in 2 quarts water until soft. Remove from broth and cool enough so meat can be taken from bone and cut into small pieces. Return meat to broth.
2. Add all other ingredients plus water enough to cover. Cook until vegetables are tender, about 20 minutes. Add additional salt and pepper to taste.

Any vegetable in season can be used – corn, peas, lima beans, yellow beans, etc.

Chilly Day Soup

1 large carrot   Makes 6-8 servings
2 cups water
2 large onions
1 quart diced potatoes
2 Tbsp. rice
⅓ cup macaroni
1 tsp. salt
¼ tsp. pepper
2 cups milk
2 Tbsp. butter

1. Chop carrot and cook in 2 cups water. While cooking chop onions.
2. When carrot is partially cooked add onions, potatoes, rice, macaroni, salt, and pepper. Add enough water to cover and cook until tender.
3. Add milk and butter and heat thoroughly.

Variations:
   1. Add 2 cups chicken broth in place of milk and butter.
   2. Add 1 cup cooked meat to soup when milk is added.

Old Time Beef Stew

Makes 6 servings

2 lbs. beef cubes
2 Tbsp. shortening
1 large onion, sliced
4 cups boiling water or tomato juice
1 Tbsp. salt
1 Tbsp. lemon juice
1 Tbsp. sugar
1 Tbsp. worcestershire sauce
½ Tbsp. pepper
½ Tbsp. paprika
dash of allspice or ground cloves
6 carrots cut in quarters
6 potatoes cut in chunks
½ cup cold water
¼ cup flour

1. Brown beef cubes in shortening for about 20 minutes. Add onion, water, salt, lemon juice, sugar, worcestershire sauce, pepper, paprika, and allspice or cloves. Cover and simmer 2 hours. Stir occasionally to prevent sticking.
2. Add vegetables. Simmer 30 minutes longer.
3. Combine water and flour. Stir until smooth. Pull vegetables and meat to one side of pan. Add flour mixture and

stir until gravy is thickened.

Variation:
    Add 1½ cups green beans with vegetables.

Soups

Delicious Vegetable Soup

2 Tbsp. butter   Makes 4-6 servings
1 onion, chopped
1 lb. hamburger
1½ tsp. salt
1 cup carrots, diced
½ cup celery, chopped
1 cup potatoes, diced
2 cups tomato juice
2 cups milk
¼ cup flour

1. Brown meat and onion in butter. Add remaining ingredients except milk and flour and cook until vegetables are tender.
2. Combine milk and flour and stir until smooth. Add to soup and cook until thickened.

from
Amish and Mennonite
kitchens

Beef or Chicken Noodle Soup

Beef soup bone or   Makes 6 servings
     boney chicken parts
1 celery stalk, chopped
1 onion, chopped
½ lb. noodles
salt and pepper

1. Cook beef or chicken with onion and celery in 3 quarts water until meat is tender. Remove meat from broth and pick from bones.
2. Add noodles to boiling broth and cook until tender. Return meat to soup. Salt and pepper to taste.

Ham Noodle Soup

1 ham bone   Makes 6 servings
1 Tbsp. onion, chopped
1 celery stalk, chopped
½ lb. noodles
salt and pepper

1. Cook ham bone, onion, and celery in 3 quarts of water until meat is tender.

Remove meat from broth and pick from bone.
2. Add noodles to boiling broth and cook until tender. Return meat to soup. Salt and pepper to taste.

Chili Con Carne

2 Tbsp. shortening	Makes 6 servings

2 Tbsp. shortening
1 onion, diced
1 clove garlic (optional)
1 lb. ground beef
1½ tsp. salt
1 Tbsp. flour
2½ tsp. chili powder
2 cups tomatoes
1 cup hot water
3 cups cooked kidney beans

1. Melt shortening and sauté onion and garlic. Add hamburger. Brown meat and sprinkle with salt, flour, and chili powder.
2. Add tomatoes and hot water. Cover and simmer for 1 hour.
3. Add kidney beans and heat thoroughly.

from
*Amish and Mennonite
kitchens*

Creamy Potato Soup

3 Tbsp. butter   Makes 4-6 servings
1 onion, diced
4 large potatoes, cubed
3 Tbsp. parsley, chopped
3 stalks celery and leaves, chopped
2 large carrots, chopped or grated
2 tsp. salt
¼ tsp. paprika
1½ cups boiling water
White sauce

1. Sauté onion in butter until tender. Add remaining ingredients except white sauce and cook until vegetables are tender.
2. Add white sauce and stir until blended.

White Sauce

4 cups milk
2 Tbsp. flour
4 Tbsp. butter
2 chicken bouillon cubes
1 tsp. salt
¼ tsp. pepper

1. Mix ½ cup milk with flour. Heat

remaining milk to boiling. Add flour mixture and stir constantly until thickened. Add remaining ingredients and stir until bouillon cubes are dissolved.

Potato Soup with Rivels

¼ cup butter   Makes 5 servings
10-12 medium potatoes, peeled and diced
salt and pepper to taste
Rivels (see page 48 for directions)

1. In saucepan combine butter, potatoes, salt, and pepper. Cover with water. Bring to a boil. Add rivels. Cook until potatoes are tender. Sprinkle with parsley leaves before serving.

"You don't even need crackers with this!"

Potato Soup

¼ cup celery, diced   Makes 6-8 servings
3 cups water
2 cups potatoes, diced
1 medium onion, chopped
salt and pepper to taste
1 quart milk
2 Tbsp. butter
3 hard-boiled eggs, chopped

1. Boil celery in 1 cup of water. When partially soft add remaining water, potatoes, onion, salt, and pepper. Cook until tender.
2. Add milk and chopped eggs. Heat thoroughly. Add butter and serve.

Variations:
1. When potatoes, onion, and celery are soft, put in blender with half of the milk which has been heated. Add ½ cup grated cheese and blend until smooth. Add remaining hot milk and butter and stir. Garnish with chopped or shredded hard-boiled eggs.
2. Add 1 diced carrot to vegetables while cooking. Garnish with parsley flakes.

Potato Soup with Sausage Balls

2 Tbsp. margarine   Makes 4 servings
1 small onion, chopped
1 stalk celery, chopped
3 or 4 potatoes, diced
½ lb. loose pork sausage formed into
    small balls about 1" in diameter
2 tsp. salt
1½ cup water
1 egg
3 cups milk

1. Sauté onion and celery in butter. Add potatoes, sausage balls, salt, and water and cook until potatoes are tender.
2. Break egg into potato mixture and stir with fork until cooked.
3. Add milk and heat thoroughly.

from
Amish and Mennonite
kitchens

Oyster and Potato Stew

Makes 4 servings

2 medium potatoes, diced
1 celery stalk, chopped
salt
1½ cups water
1½ dozen stewing oysters
¼ tsp. salt
3 cups milk
1 Tbsp. butter
pepper

1. Cook potatoes and celery in 1 cup of water until tender. Salt to taste.
2. In the remaining ½ cup water, cook the oysters with ¼ tsp. salt. Heat until boiling and the oysters begin to curl.
3. Add milk, butter, and vegetables. Heat thoroughly. Add pepper to taste.

Oyster Stew

1 quart milk
1 pint stewing oysters
2 Tbsp. butter
1 tsp. salt
dash of pepper

Makes 4 servings

1. In a 2 quart saucepan heat milk to the boiling point.
2. In a frying pan melt the butter and brown it.
3. Drain the oysters; then add them one at a time to the browned butter. Cook for only 2 to 3 minutes. Add the salt.
4. Add the oysters and butter to the hot milk and serve at once.

"Don't overcook oysters — and you'll have tender meat and a flavorful broth."

Clam Stew

Makes 6 servings

¼ cup butter or
    margarine
1 medium onion, minced
½ cup celery, finely chopped
4 potatoes, diced
½ tsp. salt
2 cups water
12 clams or
    2 8 oz. cans of clams, chopped
3 Tbsp. flour
1 quart milk
3 hard boiled eggs, diced

1. Melt butter or margarine; sauté
onion and celery until soft but not brown.
2. Add potatoes and salt. Cover with 2
cups water. Simmer until soft.
3. Add clams with their juices and cook
an additional 10 minutes.
4. Stir in the flour. Gradually add milk
and cook slowly until mixture thickens.
5. Stir in eggs just before serving.

Salmon Chowder

3-4 potatoes, diced   Makes 6 servings
2 Tbsp. onion, minced
2 Tbsp. celery, chopped
1 lb. canned salmon (remove skin and
    bones), flaked
1 cup corn
1 tsp. salt
pinch pepper
1 quart milk
2 Tbsp. butter

1. Combine potatoes, onion, and celery in saucepan. Add water enough to cover and cook until vegetables are tender.
2. Add salmon, corn, salt, pepper, and milk. Heat slowly. Add butter and serve with crackers.

"A simple, quick, and satisfying meal."

Soups

Celery Chowder

1 large onion, diced   Makes 4-6 servings
1 Tbsp. butter
3 cups green celery, chopped
1 cup potatoes, diced
4 cups milk
2 hard-boiled eggs, chopped
salt and pepper to taste

1. Sauté onion in butter until soft. Add celery and potatoes. Cover with water and cook until soft.
2. Add milk and eggs and heat thoroughly. Salt and pepper to taste.

Broccoli and Cauliflower Soup

2 cups broccoli   Makes 4 servings
2 cups cauliflower
½ cup water
1 tsp. salt
½ tsp. basil
2 Tbsp. butter
2½ Tbsp. flour
3 cups milk

1. In saucepan combine broccoli, cauliflower,

water, salt, and basil. Cook until tender.
2. In separate pan melt butter until lightly browned. Add flour and stir until smooth. Gradually add milk, stirring constantly until thickened. Pour over vegetable mixture and stir until blended.

Cream of Broccoli Soup

1¼ lb. broccoli   Makes 8 servings
4 Tbsp. butter
¼ cup mushrooms, chopped
1 Tbsp. onion, chopped
4 Tbsp. flour
3½ cups milk
1 lb. sharp cheddar cheese, grated
1 tsp. salt

1. Cook broccoli. Chop and set aside.
2. Melt butter in large, heavy pan. Add mushrooms and onion. Sauté until tender.
3. Add flour and stir until bubbly.
4. Gradually add 1½ cups milk, stirring constantly to prevent lumps. Add cheese and stir until smooth. Add remaining milk.
5. Add broccoli and heat thoroughly.

Ham and Cabbage Soup

2 Tbsp. butter or margarine   Makes 6 servings

¼ cup onion, minced

¼ cup celery, chopped

¼ cup flour

½ tsp. salt

⅛ tsp. pepper

3 cups water

2 cups cabbage, chopped or shredded

2 cups ham, cooked and diced

¾ cup dairy sour cream

1. Melt butter; then sauté onion and celery until tender. Add flour, salt, and pepper, blending till smooth.
2. Add water and cook until mixture comes to a boil, stirring constantly.
3. Add cabbage. Cover and simmer until cabbage is tender, about 10 minutes.
4. Stir in ham and cook until heated through.
5. Blend in sour cream. Heat, but do not boil.

Cream of Onion Soup

2 Tbsp. margarine   Makes 6 servings
4 Tbsp. flour
2 cups chicken stock
4 cups milk
4 Tbsp. margarine
1 cup onion, chopped
½ tsp. salt
¼ tsp. pepper
¼ cup parsley
4 Tbsp. cream

1. Melt 2 Tbsp. of margarine. Add flour and stir until smooth.
2. Add chicken stock, stirring constantly until smooth and thickened. Gradually add milk. Continue stirring until mixture comes to the boiling point, then set soup aside.
3. In a separate pan sauté onion in 4 Tbsp. of margarine. When tender add seasonings and cream. Simmer gently for 15 minutes.
4. Add onion mixture to soup. Heat but do not boil.

Soups

Tomato Soup

2 cups tomato juice Makes 4-6 servings
  (home canned with peppers, onion, and
  celery)
½ tsp. baking soda
1 quart milk
1 tsp. salt
dash of pepper
2 Tbsp. butter

1. Heat tomato juice to boiling. When boiling add baking soda and stir quickly because mixture will foam. Remove from heat.
2. Meanwhile, heat milk. Do not boil. Add salt, pepper, and butter. When milk is hot, add hot tomato mixture to it. Serve soup with crackers.

"We used to eat this with toasted cheese sandwiches for lunch. Now I like to serve it as an appetizer."

Bean Soup

2 cups dried navy beans   Makes 8 servings
1 ham bone
2 quarts water
salt and pepper
2 quarts milk
3 Tbsp. butter

1. Soak beans overnight in enough water to cover. In the morning, drain beans. Add water and ham bone. Cook slowly until meat and beans are soft. Pick meat from bone. Chop and return to bean mixture.
2. Add milk. Heat thoroughly. Season with salt and pepper to taste. Add butter and serve.

Variations:
1. Add ½ cup chopped onion.
2. Add ½ cup chopped celery.
3. Add ½ cup chopped carrot.

Soups

Pea Soup

1 quart peas
(fresh or frozen)   *Makes 8 servings*
3 quarts milk
Rivels (see page 48 for directions)
1 tsp. pepper
6 hard-boiled eggs, sliced
¼ lb. butter

1. Cook peas until tender. In separate pan bring to boil 1 quart of milk.
2. Make rivels and drop by small amounts from the back of a spoon into the boiling milk. Boil 5-7 minutes.
3. Add remaining milk and salt. Add pepper, eggs, peas, and butter. Heat thoroughly.

"The rivels make this one stick to your ribs!"

Split Pea Soup

1 lb. dried split peas   Makes 6-8 servings
2 quarts water
1 ham hock
1 cup celery, finely chopped
1 medium onion, finely chopped
2 carrots, finely chopped or shredded
salt and pepper to taste

1. Combine peas and water. Bring to a boil and boil 2 minutes. Remove from heat. Cover and let set for 1 hour.
2. Add remaining ingredients. Bring to boiling point. Reduce heat and simmer 2½-3 hours until peas look creamed and ham hock is tender. Remove ham hock. Trim meat from bone and dice. Return meat to soup. Heat thoroughly and serve.

Additional water or milk may be added to soup for a thinner consistency.

Soups

from
Amish and Mennonite
kitchens

Cold Bread Soup

Cut bread in chunks or cubes. Sugar to taste and pour cold milk over bread and sugar.

Huckleberries, cherries, or peaches in season can be added. Serve in large soup bowl.

Coffee Soup

Break 1 piece of bread into a cup. Fill cup with hot coffee; add sugar and cream to taste.

"These recipes probably came about during the Depression. But I still get hungry for a bowl of Coffee or Cold Bread Soup at breakfast or lunch!"

Stewed Crackers and Soft-Cooked Eggs

¼ - ½ lb. (about 50 or 60) buttermilk, saltine, or round soup crackers

Makes 4-5 servings

2 ½ cups milk
2 Tbsp. butter or margarine
4 or 5 eggs

1. Butter bottom and sides of a 1½ quart casserole. Lay dry crackers in casserole.
2. Heat milk to scalding. Pour over crackers. Cover casserole and let stand at least 5 minutes, checking once to make sure crackers are in the milk.
3. Just before serving, heat butter until browned and pour over crackers.
4. Cook the eggs separately (4 minutes in boiling water), and serve with the crackers, breaking an egg over each person's mound of crackers or along side.

Soups

Stewed Pretzels

pretzels
2 Tbsp. butter
1½ cups milk

1. Fill a covered 1½ quart dish about half full of broken pretzels. (Thicker pretzels are better than thin ones or pretzel sticks). Pour boiling water to level of pretzels. Let soak at least ½ hour. When pretzels are soft drain off any excess water.
2. Melt butter and allow it to brown. Add milk. Bring to boil. Pour hot milk over pretzels. Replace cover and allow to stand 5-10 minutes before serving.

"It's a good way to use stale pretzels!"

Rice Soup

1 2 lb. beef soup bone
3 tsp. salt
¼ tsp. pepper
2 quarts beef broth
1 cup rice
Rivels (see page 48 for directions)

Makes 8-10 servings

1. Boil soup bone with salt and pepper in enough water to cover, until tender. Remove meat from bone and set aside. Measure broth and add water if needed to equal 2 quarts.
2. Add rice to broth and cook 15-20 minutes until rice is tender.
3. Add rivels to soup. Add meat. Boil slowly for about 7 minutes.

"We like it very much. It's quite hearty and suits my farmer husband quite well."

Salads

from
Amish and Mennonite
kitchens

Salads

The choice food today for nutritionally conscious eaters, salads have been on the menu in Pennsylvania Dutch homes as long as meat and potatoes.

When gardens are abundant with greens, there are salads for lunch and supper in any number of combinations. The freshly bright flavors are bound together with only the mildest cream dressings.

Company for dinner or a covered dish occasion call for salads that are crafted "events." Fruits, vegetables, and nuts are treated royally.

Here are salads to serve as a vegetable, a main dish, or nearly a dessert. All offer a refreshing, light taste. All marry nature's flavors in a refreshing fashion.

Fall Fruit Salad

2 cups raw cranberries, ground   Makes 10-12 servings

3 cups miniature marshmallows

¾ cup sugar

2 cups unpeeled apples, diced

½ cup seedless white or green grapes

½ cup broken walnuts

¼ tsp. salt

1 cup heavy cream, whipped

1. Combine cranberries, marshmallows, and sugar. Cover and chill overnight.
2. Add apples, grapes, walnuts, and salt. Fold in whipped cream. Chill.
3. Turn into serving bowl or spoon onto individual lettuce leaves. Garnish with white or green grapes.

Salads

Broccoli Salad

2 bunches of broccoli, cut in bite-sized pieces
2 medium red onions, sliced thin
¼ cup raisins
8 slices bacon, fried and crumbled
1 cup mayonnaise
¼ cup sugar
2 Tbsp. vinegar

Makes 10-12 servings

1. Mix broccoli, onions, raisins, and bacon together gently.
2. Blend mayonnaise, sugar, and vinegar thoroughly.
3. Fold dressing into vegetable mixture and refrigerate 1 to 2 hours before serving.

Variations:
1. Sprinkle finished salad with 1 cup shredded cheese.
2. Add ½ lb. fresh mushrooms, sliced, to salad.
3. Substitute ½ cup shredded purple cabbage in place of onions.

Spinach Salad

1 lb. fresh spinach   Makes 6~8 servings
¼ lb. fresh, raw mushrooms
¼ cup scallions, sliced thin
1 green pepper, chopped
2 hard~cooked eggs, diced
6~8 strips of bacon, fried and crumbled

1. Tear washed and drained spinach in bite~sized pieces.
2. Toss gently with remaining ingredients.

Dressing

2 Tbsp. hot bacon drippings
½ cup salad oil
3 Tbsp. cider vinegar
3 Tbsp. honey

1. Mix all ingredients together well.
2. Pour over tossed salad and serve immediately.

Salads

Seven-Layer Salad

Makes 18-20 servings

1 medium head of lettuce, torn into bite-sized pieces
1 cup celery, diced
4 hard-boiled eggs, sliced
10 oz. frozen peas, uncooked and separated
½ cup green pepper, diced
1 onion, sliced thin
1½ cups mayonnaise
2 Tbsp. sugar
4 oz. cheddar cheese, grated
8 slices bacon, fried and crumbled
parsley

1. In large bowl layer lettuce, followed by celery, then eggs, peas, peppers, and onion.
2. Combine mayonnaise and sugar and spread over vegetables. Sprinkle with cheese.
3. Cover and refrigerate 8 to 12 hours.
4. Sprinkle with crumbled bacon and parsley before serving. To serve, toss the salad, or serve it layered as prepared.

Winter Vegetable Salad

1 head cauliflower, chopped   Makes 20~22 servings
1 bunch broccoli, chopped
3 carrots, sliced
2 cucumbers, sliced
15~20 radishes, sliced
1 small onion, sliced thin

Gently toss together all ingredients in mixing bowl. Top with dressing. Chill before serving.

Dressing

1 cup sour cream
1 cup mayonnaise
¼ tsp. garlic salt
¼ tsp. chives
¼ tsp. basil
¼ tsp. oregano

Combine and pour over vegetables.

"If you serve this salad to herb lovers, increase the chives, basil, and oregano to ½ tsp. each!"

Dandelion Salad

a dishpan full of young dandelion stalks	Makes 4-6 servings

4 strips bacon
½ cup sugar
2 Tbsp. flour
1 egg, beaten
1 tsp. salt
½ cup vinegar
1½ cups water
3 hard-boiled eggs, diced

1. Wash, drain, and cut up tender dandelion leaves.
2. Brown bacon; remove from drippings and crumble.
3. Combine sugar and flour. Add egg, salt, vinegar, and water and mix until smooth.
4. Pour into bacon drippings and heat, stirring constantly, until mixture thickens.
5. Pour warm dressing over dandelion. Add crumbled bacon and hard-boiled eggs. Toss lightly and serve immediately.

Variation:
Use fresh endive instead of dandelion.

Cabbage Slaw

    6 cups cabbage,   Makes 14-16 servings
       shredded
    1 cup carrot, shredded
    ¼ cup green pepper, chopped

1. Combine cabbage, carrot, and pepper. and chill.
2. Blend dressing. Stir lightly into vegetable mixture.

Dressing

    1 cup mayonnaise
    2 Tbsp. sugar
    2 Tbsp. vinegar
    1 tsp. prepared mustard
    1 tsp. celery seed

Blend well and pour over vegetables.

Salads

Leaf Lettuce Salad

a serving bowl or   Makes 4 servings
    half a dishpan full of cutting lettuce
1 cup whipping cream
2 Tbsp. sugar
2 Tbsp. brown sugar
3 Tbsp. vinegar
pinch of salt
3 hard-boiled eggs, diced
dash of paprika

1. Wash and drain lettuce well.
2. Whip cream until it is stiff but doesn't form peaks.
3. Blend sugars, vinegar, and salt. Fold into whipped cream.
4. Pour over lettuce. Toss; then garnish with egg and sprinkles of paprika.

French Dressing

½ cup salad oil   Makes 2 cups
¾ cup sugar
¼ cup apple vinegar
½ cup ketchup
1 small onion, minced

1½ tsp. paprika
1 tsp. celery seed

Put all ingredients in blender and mix until smooth.

Celery Seed Salad Dressing

1 cup sugar   Makes 1½ pints
2 tsp. dry mustard
2 tsp. salt
2 tsp. paprika
½ cup vinegar
2 cups salad oil
2 tsp. celery seed
1 Tbsp. grated onion

1. Combine first 5 ingredients and stir well.
2. Add the oil very slowly and beat well.
3. Stir in onion and celery seed.
4. Let dressing stand 24 hours before using.

Salads

from
Amish and Mennonite
kitchens

Marinated Carrots

2 lbs. whole carrots   Makes 8 servings
1 large onion, sliced in thin rings
1 green pepper, sliced
1 cup tomato juice
1 cup sugar
1 cup vegetable oil
1 tsp. dry mustard
¾ cup vinegar
1 tsp. salt
½ tsp. pepper

1. Cook whole carrots until just softened. Slice them into ¾"-1" chunks. Stir in the onion rings and green pepper slices.
2. Whisk together the remaining 7 ingredients until well blended. Pour over the vegetables and let mixture marinate overnight.
3. Serve chilled.

Green Bean Salad

6 slices bacon, fried and crumbled
1 lb. fresh or 1 pint cooked green beans
¼ tsp. salt
½ cup celery, chopped fine

2 - 3 hard-cooked eggs, chopped
1 small onion, chopped fine
pickles, chopped fine (optional)

1. Fry bacon until crisp; then crumble. Add green beans, small amount of water, and salt to bacon drippings. Cook just until tender.
2. Mix with celery, eggs, onion, pickles, if desired. Stir in dressing; then serve hot or cold.

Dressing
1 Tbsp. onion, grated
⅓ cup vinegar
2 Tbsp. sugar
½ tsp. salt
dash of pepper, paprika, and
    garlic powder

Heat together until boiling. Pour over green beans immediately or chill and serve over cold beans.

Salads

Three-Bean Salad

1 pint green beans,   Makes 12 servings
   cooked
1 pint yellow wax beans, cooked
1 pint kidney beans, cooked and rinsed
1 purple onion, sliced thin
½ cup celery, diced
½ cup red or green pepper, diced

1. Drain all the beans well and mix together. Then stir in the onion, celery, and pepper.
2. Stir in dressing. Let stand several hours or overnight to allow the flavor to blend.

Dressing

¾ cup sugar
⅔ cup vinegar
⅓ cup salad oil
1 tsp. salt
¼ tsp. pepper

Blend together thoroughly; then pour over vegetables.

Cucumbers and Onions

Salads

Makes 4-6 servings

2 medium
   cucumbers
2 medium onions
salt
2-3 Tbsp. mayonnaise
1 Tbsp. sugar
1 Tbsp. vinegar

1. Peel cucumbers and slice thin. Layer in shallow dish, sprinkling each layer with salt. Let stand overnight.
2. In the morning, drain cucumbers and rinse. Let dry on paper towels.
3. Slice onions thin. Mix gently with cucumber slices.
4. Beat together the mayonnaise, sugar, and vinegar until creamy. Stir into mixed cucumbers and onions. (The dressing should be plentiful so the salad is creamy. Increase amounts of dressing ingredients, proportionally, if needed.)

Potato Salad

Makes 10 servings

6 medium-sized potatoes
1 small onion, chopped fine
1 cup celery, chopped
1 tsp. celery seed
1 tsp. salt
4 hard-cooked eggs, diced

1. Cook potatoes in their jackets until soft. Peel and dice.
2. Mix potatoes gently with the remaining five ingredients; then add to the Dressing.

Dressing

2 eggs, well beaten
¾ cup sugar
1 tsp. cornstarch
salt to taste
¼ - ½ cup vinegar
½ cup cream or evaporated milk
1 tsp mustard
3 Tbsp. butter, softened
1 cup mayonnaise

1. Mix eggs with sugar, cornstarch and

salt. Add vinegar, cream, and mustard. Cook until thickened.

2. Remove from heat and beat in butter. Add mayonnaise and mix until smooth.

3. Add potatoe mixture to the cooled dressing, folding gently together.

Salads

Sunset Salad

Makes 6 servings

1 3 oz. package
     orange gelatin
½ tsp. salt
1 cup boiling water
1 cup cold pineapple juice
1 Tbsp. lemon juice or vinegar
1 cup crushed pineapple, drained
1 cup carrots coarsely grated

1. Dissolve gelatin and salt in boiling water. Add pineapple juice and lemon juice. Refrigerate until mixture begins to jell.

2. Fold in pineapple and carrots. Return to refrigerator until fully jelled.

3. Cut into squares and serve on a lettuce leaf.

from
Amish and Mennonite
kitchens

Macaroni Salad

1 lb. macaroni   Makes 20 servings
   (or baby sea shells)
1½ cup celery, chopped
½ cup carrots, finely grated
¼ cup onion, finely chopped
6 hard-cooked eggs, sliced
paprika

1. Cook macaroni as directed, drain, and cool.
2. Set aside 1 hard-cooked egg; then stir together gently the cooked macaroni, celery, carrots, onion, and remaining eggs.

Dressing

1 pint miracle whip
¼ cup vinegar
¾ cup sugar
2 Tbsp. prepared mustard

1. Blend together; then fold into macaroni salad mixture.
2. Garnish with 1 hard-cooked egg and paprika.

Ham Salad

2½ lb. ham, chopped or ground

Makes 20 servings

1½ dozen eggs, hard-cooked and chopped

Mix together lightly.

Dressing

1 cup sugar
¾ cup vinegar
1 egg, beaten
1½ Tbsp. flour
½ tsp. salt
1 tsp. prepared mustard
1 cup milk

1. Heat sugar and vinegar to the boiling point. Add the remaining ingredients, stirring until smooth. Cook till thickened. Cool.
2. Stir dressing into ham and eggs.
3. Serve on lettuce or in sandwiches.

Salads

from
Amish and Mennonite
kitchens

Apple Delight Salad

8 unpeeled apples,   Makes 10 servings
   diced
½ cup celery, chopped
½ cup raisins
½ cup broken walnuts
1 cup miniature marshmallows, optional

Stir above ingredients together, gently.

Dressing
1 Tbsp. cornstarch
1 cup water
1 tsp. vinegar
¼ tsp. salt
½ cup sugar
¼ cup rich milk or cream
1 tsp. vanilla

1. Blend cornstarch into water. Stir in other ingredients over low heat until all are dissolved. Bring to boiling point.
2. Cool and pour over apple mixture. Chill. Garnish with parsley to serve.

Apples and Friends

6 apples, unpared, chopped
1 dozen large marshmallows, chopped
1 dozen dates, seeded and chopped
4 bananas, sliced
½ cup nuts, chopped

1. Stir all ingredients together gently.
2. Cover with dressing, mix, and chill before serving.

Dressing

⅓ cup sugar
½ cup cream
½ cup milk
1 Tbsp. butter
1 egg
1 Tbsp. vinegar
1 tsp. prepared mustard
1 tsp. salad dressing

1. Mix together the sugar, cream, milk, butter, and egg. Bring to a boil.
2. Remove from heat and stir in vinegar, mustard, and salad dressing.
3. Cool; then pour over fruit.

Salads

97

Golden Fruit Dish

3 large Golden   Makes 10 servings
    Delicious (or any other yellow
    variety) apples
4 large ripe bananas
1~1lb. can unsweetened crushed pineapple
½ cup undiluted frozen orange juice,
    unsweetened

1. Dice or grate the apples. Slice the bananas.
2. Stir the fruits together, adding the pineapple and softened orange juice concentrate.
Mix thoroughly.
3. Chill overnight to allow flavors to blend.

"May be served as a salad or dessert."

Tropical Fruit Mold

1 3oz. package   Makes 18~20 servings
    lemon jello
2 cups hot water or fruit juice
22 large marshmallows
6 oz. Philadelphia cream cheese
1 Tbsp. salad dressing
1 cup pineapple chunks, chopped

1 cup celery, chopped
1 cup nuts, broken
1 cup whipping cream, whipped
1 6 oz. package cherry jello
2 cups hot water
2 cups cold water

1. Dissolve lemon jello in hot water or fruit juice. Then add the marshmallows and stir until they are dissolved.
2. Mix cream cheese and salad dressing together until softened; then add to the jello mixture. Finally, add the pineapple chunks.
3. When the above mixture begins to jell, fold in the celery, nuts, and whipped cream. Pour into a 9"x 13" baking dish and chill until set.
4. Dissolve the cherry jello in hot water; then add the cold water.
5. When the cherry jello begins to congeal, spoon on top of yellow salad layer. When completely set, cut into 2½" squares and serve on lettuce leaves.

Rhubarb Salad

2 cups rhubarb,   Makes 8-10 servings
  diced
½ cup sugar
¼ cup water
1 ~ 6 oz. package strawberry gelatin
2 cups boiling water
1 Tbsp. lemon juice
1 banana, sliced
3 oz. Philadelphia cream cheese, cut
  in cubes

1. Cook the rhubarb, sugar and ¼ cup water together for 5 minutes. Set aside and cool.
2. Dissolve strawberry gelatin in 2 cups boiling water. Let cool.
3. Fold rhubarb mixture, banana, and cubed cream cheese into slightly thickened gelatin.
4. Pour into mold and chill until set.

Lemon - Orange Sauce

    1 egg, beaten
    ½ tsp. lemon rind
    ½ tsp. orange rind
    2 Tbsp. lemon juice
    ⅓ cup sugar
    ½ pint whipping cream, whipped

1. Combine the egg, lemon and orange rinds, lemon juice, and sugar together in a sauce pan and cook 3 minutes. Cool.
2. Fold whipped cream into the sauce mixture. Chill. Serve over the unmolded rhubarb salad.

Cider Salad Mold

Makes 10-12 servings

4 cups apple cider
4 whole cloves
4 inch cinnamon stick
1 6 oz. package lemon gelatin
1 orange, peeled and sectioned
1 unpeeled apple, cored and diced

1. In saucepan combine cider, cloves, and cinnamon. Simmer covered for 15 minutes, then strain.
2. Dissolve gelatin in hot cider. Pour 1 cup of the cider mixture into 5½ cup mold. Chill until partially set. Keep remaining gelatin at room temperature.
3. Arrange orange sections over first layer of gelatin in mold. Chill till almost firm.
4. Meanwhile, chill remaining gelatin till partially set. Fold in apple. Carefully pour gelatin with apple over orange layer. Chill until firm.
5. Unmold, surround with lettuce leaves, and serve with mayonnaise.

Cinnamon Applesauce Salad

¾ cup red cinnamon candies

Makes 8~10 servings

1 cup hot water

1 ~ 3 oz. package red raspberry gelatin

1½ cups applesauce

1 ~ 8 oz. package Philadelphia Cream Cheese, softened

½ cup mayonnaise

½ cup celery, chopped

1. Add cinnamon candies to hot water. Bring to a boil, stirring to dissolve.
2. Pour over gelatin, stirring until the gelatin is dissolved. Add applesauce and blend well.
3. Pour half of this mixture into mold that has been rubbed with mayonnaise and chill until set
4. Mix together well the softened cream cheese, mayonnaise, and celery and spread over the set gelatin mixture.
5. Pour remaining gelatin mixture on top and chill until set. Unmold to serve.

Salads

Apricot Salad

Makes 18 servings

- 6 oz. package apricot gelatin
- 1 cup hot water
- 2 cups cold water or fruit juice
- 20 oz. can apricots, drained and cut in small pieces
- 20 oz. can crushed pineapple, drained
- 1 cup miniature marshmallows
- whipped cream

1. Dissolve gelatin in hot water. Add cold water or juice. Cool until slightly thickened.
2. Add remaining ingredients and pour into a 9"x13" pan. Chill until firm.
3. Cut into squares and dollop with whipped cream to serve.

Fruited Jello Mold

- 1 cup cold water
- 2 envelopes unflavored gelatin
- 2/3 cup sugar
- 1/8 tsp. salt
- 2 cups ice cubes
- 1/2 cup lemon juice

4 cups mixed fruit – apples, pears, peaches, grapes (seeded), apricots, cherries (seeded), bananas, oranges, or any combination of these.

1. Pour water into saucepan. Sprinkle in gelatin. Place over moderate heat and stir until the gelatin is dissolved. Remove from heat; add sugar and salt and stir until dissolved.
2. Add ice and lemon juice, stirring until the cubes are melted or until the mixture is the consistency of egg whites.
3. Fold in fruit and put in 6 cup mold. Chill until firm. Unmold to serve.

Variation:
   Use 2 cups ginger ale in place of 2 cups ice cubes. Mixture will then need to be refrigerated to reach egg-white consistency before adding fruit.

Creamy Cheese and Fruit Mold

Makes 10 servings

3 oz. package orange gelatin
¾ cup hot water
3 oz. package Philadelphia cream cheese, softened
1 cup vanilla ice cream, softened
¾ cup cottage cheese
1 cup crushed pineapple, drained
1 can mandarin oranges, drained
½ cup pecan pieces
whole pecans, optional

1. Dissolve gelatin in hot water. Then blend in cream cheese, ice cream, and cottage cheese. Chill until partially set.
2. Stir in fruit and nuts. Pour into mold and chill until firm.
3. To serve, unmold and garnish with whole pecans, if desired.

Cranberry Salad

1 ~ 3 oz. package   Makes 8 servings
    cherry or strawberry gelatin
1 cup hot water
½ cup cold water
½ lb. cranberries
3 apples
2 oranges or ½ cup crushed pineapple
¼ cup nuts, chopped
¾ cup sugar

1. Dissolve gelatin in hot water, then add cold water. Cool mixture and set aside.
2. Wash and grind cranberries. Pare and chop apples into small chunks.
3. Stir together the ground cranberries, chopped apples and oranges (or pineapple), nuts, and sugar.
4. Add to slightly thickened gelatin mixture; then pour into a mold and chill until salad is firm and holds its shape. Unmold on salad greens.

Salads

Vegetables

from
Amish and Mennonite
kitchens

Vegetables

Gardens and their fruits are believed to be gifts. And they're treated as such.

Because many Pennsylvania Dutch cooks are gardeners, vegetables are in abundance — fresh during the summer; preserved during the rest of the year. Peas, beans, and potatoes are most often served gently steamed and then covered with brown butter. So their natural flavors and textures are maintained.

But we haven't forgotten baked dried corn, potato filling, fried tomatoes, home baked beans, and dozens of other traditional favorites.

Here are tenderly blended sauces and rich mixtures (sweet potato apple bake and cauliflower supreme, for example) that enhance and compliment these garden dishes. All bring beauty and nutrition to any meal.

Corn Pie

Pastry for a 2-crust pie

Makes 8-10 servings

3 cups fresh corn
1½ cups raw potatoes, diced
2 or 3 hard-boiled eggs, diced
salt and pepper to taste
2 Tbsp. flour
milk

1. Line a casserole or deep pie pan with pastry.
2. Combine corn, potatoes, and eggs and pour into pastry lined container. Add salt and pepper. Sprinkle with flour. Add enough milk to cover the vegetables.
3. Cover with top pastry. Pinch edges together to seal.
4. Bake at 425° for 30-40 minutes, until crust is browned and milk is bubbly throughout.

Variation:
    Add several slices of bacon cut into 1" pieces.

Vegetables

from
Amish and Mennonite
kitchens

Baked Dried Corn

1 cup dried corn   Makes 8 servings
3 cups milk
½ tsp. salt
2 Tbsp. sugar
2 eggs, beaten
2 Tbsp. butter

1. Grind corn in food grinder or blender. Combine with milk and allow to stand ½ hour or more. Add salt, sugar, and eggs. Mix well.
2. Pour into a buttered 1 quart casserole dish. Dot with butter. Bake at 350° for 45-60 minutes.

Scalloped Corn

3 cups fresh,   Makes 6-8 servings
   frozen, or canned corn
3 eggs, beaten
1 cup milk
1½ tsp. salt
⅛ tsp. pepper
2 Tbsp. melted butter
buttered bread crumbs

1. Combine all ingredients except bread crumbs. Mix well. Pour into buttered 1-1½ quart casserole. Sprinkle with bread crumbs.
2. Bake, uncovered, at 350° for 1½ hours.

Variations:
    1. Add 1 Tbsp. flour or cornstarch.
    2. Add 1 Tbsp. minced onion.

Corn Fritters

    2 cups fresh, grated   Makes 12 fritters
        corn
    2 eggs, beaten
    ¾ cup flour
    ¾ tsp. salt
    ¼ tsp. pepper
    1 tsp. baking powder

1. Combine corn and eggs. Add flour which has been sifted with remaining ingredients.
2. Drop corn mixture from tablespoon into 1 inch of melted shortening. Fry until golden brown on both sides, turning once.

Calico Beans

1 lb. hamburger	Makes 10 servings

¼ lb. bacon
1 medium onion, diced
1 large can pork 'n beans
1 can butter beans
1 can kidney beans
½ cup catsup
½ cup brown sugar
2 Tbsp. vinegar
½ tsp. salt

1. Brown hamburger, bacon, and onion in skillet. Combine meat and all beans. Pour into a greased casserole.
2. Combine catsup, brown sugar, vinegar, and salt. Pour over meat and beans.
3. Bake at 350° for 1 hour.

Baked Lima Beans

1 quart lima beans	Makes 4-6 servings

1 Tbsp. cornstarch
¼ cup water
½ lb. bacon
1 Tbsp. prepared mustard

3 Tbsp. brown sugar
2 Tbsp. King Syrup molasses

1. Boil beans until soft. Drain off excess water. Combine cornstarch and water and add to beans. Cook till thickened.
2. Fry bacon until crisp. Drain. Crumble and add to beans.
3. Add remaining ingredients. Pour into baking dish. Bake at 350° for 30 minutes.

Potato Puffs

1 cup mashed potatoes   Makes 12 puffs
2 eggs, beaten
¼ tsp. salt
⅓ cup flour
1 tsp. baking powder
shortening

1. Combine all ingredients except shortening and mix well. Deep fry until golden brown in hot shortening using 1 large tsp. of potato mixture for each puff.

Crispy Topped Cheese Potatoes

5 Tbsp. melted butter   Makes 4 servings
4 medium potatoes, cooked until
    almost soft
1 cup cornflakes, finely crushed
½ tsp. paprika
1 tsp. salt
1 cup shredded cheese

1. Pour 2 Tbsp. melted butter into shallow baking pan. Cut potatoes into ½" slices and place close together in pan. Brush tops with remaining butter.
2. Combine cornflakes, paprika, salt, and cheese. Sprinkle over potatoes.
3. Bake at 350° for 25 minutes.

Variations:
    1. Add a sprinkle of red pepper to cornflake mixture.
    2. Leave skins on potatoes.

Gourmet Cheese Potatoes

6 medium potatoes   Makes 6 servings
2 cups shredded cheddar cheese
¼ cup butter
1½ cups sour cream or milk
⅓ cup onion, chopped
1 tsp. salt
¼ tsp. pepper
2 Tbsp. butter
paprika

1. Cook potatoes in skins. Shred coarsely.
2. In saucepan over low heat combine cheese and butter. Stir until melted. Remove from heat and add sour cream, onion, salt, and pepper. Fold sauce into potatoes.
3. Pour into greased casserole. Dot with butter. Sprinkle with paprika.
4. Bake at 350° for 30 minutes or until bubbly throughout.

"We like the sour cream and cheese flavors."

Vegetables

Libby's Spinach Potatoes

1 10 oz. pkg. frozen   Makes 6 servings
    spinach
6-8 large potatoes, cooked and mashed
¾ cup sour cream
2 tsp. salt
1 tsp. sugar
¼ tsp. pepper
2 tsp. chopped chives
¼ tsp. dill weed
4 Tbsp. butter or margarine melted
1 cup grated cheese

1. Thaw and drain spinach.
2. Combine all ingredients except cheese.
Mix well. Place in greased casserole and
top with cheese.
3. Bake at 400° for 20 minutes.

"This is good, nutritious, and uses
ingredients I'm likely to have on hand."

Potato Fritters

4 cups mashed potatoes
    Makes about 10 fritters
2 eggs, well beaten
2 Tbsp. parsley, finely chopped
½ onion, finely chopped
¼ cup pimento, minced
2 tsp. baking powder
flour

1. Combine all ingredients and mix well. Flour may be added if needed so potatoes can be shaped. Fritters may be fried like pancakes in a skillet or dropped by spoonfuls into hot fat. If enough flour is added potatoes can be formed into balls and rolled in crushed cornflakes before deep frying.

"An interesting way to use leftover mashed potatoes."

Vegetables

Mashed Potato Filling

½ cup butter   Makes 10 servings
½ cup celery, chopped
2 Tbsp. onion, chopped
4 cups soft bread cubes
1 pinch saffron
½ cup boiling water
3 eggs, beaten
2 cups milk
1½ tsp. salt
2 cups mashed potatoes

1. Melt butter. Add celery and onion. Cook until tender. Pour over bread cubes and mix well.
2. Combine saffron and boiling water. Add to bread and mix well. Add remaining ingredients to bread, mixing well after each addition. Finished product should be very moist. Add more milk if necessary.
3. Turn into 2 well greased casserole dishes. Bake at 350° for 45 minutes.

Bread Filling

Makes 6 servings

4 eggs
2 cups milk
2 quarts soft bread cubes
4 Tbsp. melted butter
1 Tbsp. parsley, chopped
1 tsp. onion, minced
1 tsp. salt
1 tsp. sage or poultry seasoning

1. Beat eggs. Add milk. Pour over bread cubes.
2. Combine butter and seasonings. Add to bread cubes and mix well.
3. Filling can be baked in a casserole dish at 350° for 45 minutes or may be used as stuffing for fowl.

"I use regular bread and break it into small pieces instead of buying bread cubes."

Vegetables

Sweet Potato Croquettes

Sweet potatoes
Bread crumbs
Margarine

1. Wash potatoes thoroughly. Cook until tender. Peel potatoes while hot. Mash them immediately with electric mixer. Beat until smooth. Potato fibers will cling to beaters.

2. Chill mashed potatoes for several hours in refrigerator. Shape potatoes into uniform croquettes approximately 3"×1¼". Roll in bread crumbs.

3. Fry croquettes in margarine, turning so all sides brown. Serve immediately. Croquettes may be frozen at this point and reheated in an oven at 325° for 20 minutes.

Variation:
    Add 3 Tbsp. brown sugar per 2 cups mashed sweet potatoes.

Sweet Potato Pudding

Makes 4-6 servings

- 2 cups mashed sweet potatoes
- 3 Tbsp. sugar
- 2 eggs, well beaten
- 2 Tbsp. melted butter
- 1 tsp. salt
- 1 cup milk
- ½ cup miniature marshmallows or marshmallow creme

1. Combine all ingredients except marshmallows. Blend well.
2. Pour into buttered casserole. Top with marshmallows.
3. Bake at 350° for 45 minutes.

You may wait to add marshmallows until the last 20 minutes of baking time. They will then be golden brown to serve.

"This is one vegetable our whole family enjoys!"

Vegetables

from
Amish and Mennonite
kitchens

Sweet Potato Apple Bake

Makes 6-8 servings

6 medium sweet
    potatoes
2 or 3 apples
¼ cup margarine
⅓ cup brown sugar
1 Tbsp. flour
1 tsp. salt
2 Tbsp. orange juice

1. Cook sweet potatoes until soft. Peel and cut in half lengthwise.
2. Peel and slice apples.
3. Combine remaining ingredients.
4. Layer ingredients in casserole making first a layer of potatoes, then apples, then half of the orange juice mixture. Repeat, topping with remaining orange juice mixture.
5. Bake at 350° for 1 hour.

"The apples really compliment the sweet potatoes."

Candied Sweet Potatoes

6 medium sweet potatoes   Makes 6 servings
salt
paprika
¾ cup brown sugar
½ tsp. grated lemon rind
1½ Tbsp. lemon juice
2 Tbsp. butter

1. Cook potatoes until soft. Peel and cut lengthwise in ½ inch slices. Place in shallow, greased baking dish. Sprinkle with salt and paprika.
2. Mix sugar, lemon rind, and lemon juice. Drizzle over potatoes.
3. Dot with butter.
4. Bake, uncovered, at 375° for 20 minutes. Baste several times during baking.

"This is an easy make-ahead dish. We used to cook the sweet potatoes Saturday night; then have them sliced and candied for Sunday lunch."

Vegetables

from
Amish and Mennonite
kitchens

Baked Rice

2 Tbsp. butter   *Makes 4 servings*
1 medium onion, chopped
1¼ cup rich beef broth
⅔ cup water
1 cup uncooked, long grain rice
slivered almonds

1. Sauté onion in butter. Add broth and water. Bring to a boil.
2. Place rice in a buttered casserole. Pour hot broth mixture over rice. Cover and bake at 350° for 40-45 minutes. Sprinkle with almonds.

Baked Carrots

2½ cups cooked,   *Makes 6-8 servings*
    mashed carrots
1 Tbsp. onion, minced
3 eggs, well beaten
2 cups rich milk
3 Tbsp. melted butter
½ cup bread crumbs
salt and pepper to taste

1. Combine all ingredients. Pour into greased casserole.
2. Bake, uncovered, at 375° for 1 hour.

Creamed Carrots

4 cups carrots, sliced   Makes 8 servings
salt and pepper to taste
3 Tbsp. butter
1 Tbsp. onion, chopped
3 Tbsp. flour
1½ cup milk
1 cup grated cheese

1. Cook carrots. Season with salt and pepper; then place in greased casserole dish.
2. Melt butter. Add onion and cook until tender. Add flour and stir until smooth. Gradually add milk, stirring constantly, and cook until thickened. Add cheese and stir until melted.
3. Pour sauce over carrots and stir gently. Bake at 350° for 30-35 minutes.

This dish is also very good with green beans.

from
Amish and Mennonite
kitchens

Green Beans with Tomatoes

1 quart cooked   Makes 6-8 servings
  green beans
4 Tbsp. butter
¼ cup onion, chopped
¼ cup green pepper, diced
1 cup canned tomatoes
1 tsp. flour
1 tsp. salt
⅛ tsp. pepper

1. Melt butter. Sauté green beans, onion, and green pepper until lightly browned.
2. Mix flour, salt, and pepper with tomatoes. Add to green bean mixture and cook slowly for 6-8 minutes.

Tomato Sauce

2 Tbsp. butter   Makes 6 servings
3 Tbsp. flour
4 Tbsp. brown sugar
1 quart canned tomatoes

1. Melt butter in heavy skillet. Add flour and stir until flour browns and mixture

becomes crumbly.

2. Add brown sugar and tomatoes with juice. Stir until mixture thickens. This may be served alone or over toast. It's a good compliment to a fish dinner.

Fried Tomatoes

3 firm, almost   *Makes 6-8 servings*
    ripe tomatoes
1 egg, beaten
2 Tbsp. milk
1 cup cracker crumbs
¼ cup shortening
salt and pepper to taste

1. Slice tomatoes into ¾ inch slices.
2. Combine egg and milk. Dip each tomato slice in egg mixture and then into cracker crumbs.
3. Melt shortening and fry coated tomato slices. Brown on both sides, turning once. Season with salt and pepper.

Peas and Knepp

1½ cups flour   Makes 10-12 servings
2 tsp. baking powder
¾ tsp. salt
3 Tbsp. shortening
¾ cup milk
6 cups fresh peas
butter

1. Combine flour, baking powder, and salt. Cut in shortening. Blend in milk.
2. Place peas in large kettle and add enough water to cover peas. Cook about 10 minutes.
3. Drop knepp dough by spoonfuls on top of boiling peas. Cook slowly for 10 minutes, uncovered. Cover with dome lid and cook 10 minutes longer. Serve drizzled with browned butter.

Knepp can be made with any vegetable in season.

Scalloped Celery and Cheese

3 cups celery, diced   Makes 6 servings
1 Tbsp. butter
3 Tbsp. flour
1½ cups milk
½ cup celery liquid
¾ tsp. salt
dash of pepper
1 cup grated cheese
1 cup buttered crumbs

1. Cook celery in water until tender. Drain, reserving ½ cup of liquid.
2. Melt butter. Add flour and stir until smooth. Gradually add milk and celery liquid. Cook, stirring constantly until thickened. Add salt, pepper, and cheese. Stir until cheese melts.
3. In greased casserole place a layer of celery, then cheese sauce, then buttered crumbs. Repeat, ending with crumbs.
4. Bake at 350° for 30-40 minutes.

Vegetables

from
Amish and Mennonite
kitchens

Cauliflower Supreme

1 head cauliflower   Makes 6-8 servings
salt to taste
2 cups tomatoes
2 Tbsp. flour
2 Tbsp. water
3 Tbsp. sugar
cheese slices

1. Break cauliflower head into pieces and cook with salt until tender. Drain well and place in greased casserole dish.
2. Put tomatoes in saucepan and bring to a boil. Make a paste of flour and water and add to tomatoes. Cook until thickened. Add sugar. Pour sauce over cauliflower. Top with slices of cheese.
3. Bake until cheese is bubbly and browned, about 30-35 minutes at 375°.

"This is a simple dish to prepare. We think it's very good!"

132

Broccoli, Cauliflower, or Asparagus with Cheese

1 head broccoli or cauliflower or 1 bunch of asparagus
cheese sauce

Makes 6-8 servings

1. Cut vegetable into pieces. Cook until soft. Drain. Serve with cheese sauce.

Cheese Sauce
    4 Tbsp. butter
    4 Tbsp. flour
    1 tsp. salt
    2 cups milk
    ½ cup cheese

1. Melt butter. Stir in flour and salt.
2. Gradually add milk, stirring constantly. Cook until smooth and thickened.
3. Add cheese and stir until melted. Pour sauce over vegetable.

Variation:
    Sprinkle buttered bread crumbs over cheese sauce.

Asparagus Loaf

Makes 8-10 servings

1 quart cooked
  asparagus
1 quart bread cubes
4 eggs
2 cups milk
2 Tbsp. melted butter
1 tsp. salt

1. Combine all ingredients. Turn into greased loaf pan or casserole dish.
2. Bake at 350° for 45-60 minutes.

Spinach with Dressing

10-12 oz. frozen spinach   Makes 4 servings
1 Tbsp. mayonnaise
1 tsp. mustard
½ tsp. sugar
¼ tsp. vinegar

1. Cook spinach. Drain.
2. Combine all other ingredients. Pour over hot spinach. Serve immediately.

Cheese-Eggplant Scallop

1 eggplant · Makes 6 servings
¼ lb. margarine
½ lb. bread cubes
2 eggs, beaten
¼ lb. grated cheese
salt and pepper to taste

1. Peel eggplant. Cut into chunks and cook in a small amount of water until tender. Drain. Mash lightly with potato masher.
2. Melt margarine. Add margarine to bread cubes. Divide bread cubes in half. To one half add eggplant, eggs, half of cheese, and salt and pepper.
3. Place half of remaining bread cubes in bottom of greased 1 quart casserole. Add eggplant mixture. Top with remaining bread cubes and sprinkle with remaining cheese.
4. Bake at 350° for 30 minutes.

Vegetables

from
Amish and Mennonite
kitchens

Fried Eggplant with Gravy

1 large eggplant   Makes 4-6 servings
flour
shortening
brown sugar
milk
salt

1. Peel eggplant and slice in ¾" slices. Dip each slice in flour to coat both sides. Sauté in small amount of shortening until browned.
2. Sprinkle each slice with brown sugar.
3. Add milk enough to cover the browned slices. Reduce heat and simmer till milk is somewhat thickened and eggplant is soft. Salt to taste.

Harvard Beets

⅓ cup sugar   Makes 6 servings
1 Tbsp. cornstarch
1 tsp. salt
¼ cup vinegar
¼ cup water

3 cups cooked beets, sliced or diced
2 Tbsp. butter

1. Combine sugar, cornstarch, and salt. Add vinegar and water. Stir until smooth. Bring mixture to a boil and cook 5 minutes.
2. Add beets to hot mixture and allow to stand for 30 minutes.
3. Just before serving bring to a boil and add butter.

Beets in Orange Sauce

1 lb. cooked sliced beets   Makes 4 servings
1½ tsp. cornstarch
½ tsp. salt
3 Tbsp. firmly packed brown sugar
½ cup orange juice
1 Tbsp. butter

1. Thoroughly drain beets.
2. In saucepan combine cornstarch, salt, and brown sugar. Gradually add orange juice. Add butter. Cook stirring constantly until thickened and clear.
3. Add beets. Heat thoroughly.

from
Amish and Mennonite
kitchens

Onion Patties

Makes 6-8 patties

¾ cup flour
2 tsp. baking powder
1 Tbsp. sugar
½ tsp. salt
1 Tbsp. corn meal
¾ cup milk
2½ cups onion, finely chopped
shortening

1. Combine dry ingredients. Add milk and mix well.
2. Stir in onions. Drop batter in small mounds into hot shortening. Fry until golden brown on both sides, turning once.

Fried Onions

Slice onions in butter in frying pan and sauté until slightly browned and tender. Add a little salt and vinegar and serve on top of potatoes boiled in their jackets.

Home Baked Beans

1 lb. Great   Makes 8-10 servings
    Northern navy beans
1 tsp. salt
½ tsp. baking soda
1 small onion, minced
2 Tbsp. molasses
½ cup brown sugar
½ cup catsup
½ lb. bacon

1. Rinse and sort beans. Cover with 3 inches of water and allow to soak overnight. In the morning, add salt and soda and bring beans to a boil. Cook for ½ hour or until tender. More water should be added if beans become dry.
2. Pour into a 2 quart casserole and add remaining ingredients. Bacon should be fried until crisp and crumbled before adding. Bacon drippings may be added for additional flavor.
3. Bake at 325° for 1½-2 hours keeping covered with liquid.

Vegetables

Meats
and Meat Dishes

from
Amish and Mennonite
kitchens

from
Amish and Mennonite
kitchens

Meats

This is hearty food. Its source is the farm. Traditionally many families have raised their own steers, hogs, and chickens. So fresh meat is at hand.

On butchering day the good cuts are frozen or canned for later use. And what happens to the rest? Some is ground into hamburger; some is turned into scrapple, bologna, or sausage, those distinctive and smoked dishes so much a part of Pennsylvania Dutch menus.

Once again their diet reflects these people's values. The meat dishes are basic - not highly seasoned, not difficult to prepare. The natural flavors are allowed to shine through. Furthermore, nothing is wasted. And simple ingenuity makes all of it tasty!

Ham Loaf

Makes 6-8 servings

- 1 lb. lean pork
- 1 lb. smoked ham
- 1 lb. ground beef
- 1 cup milk
- 1½ tsp. salt
- 1 cup bread crumbs
- 2 eggs

1. Combine all ingredients and mix well.
2. Turn into roasting pan and shape into a loaf. Bake at 350° for 1½ hours.
3. Pour sauce over ham loaf and bake an additional ½ hour.

Brown Sugar Sauce for Meat or Ham Loaf

- ¾ cup brown sugar
- 1 tsp. mustard
- ½ tsp. paprika
- ¼ cup vinegar

Combine all ingredients and mix well.

Variations:
1. Add 4 oz. crushed pineapples to sauce.
2. Use 1¼ cup cornflakes crumbs instead of bread crumbs.
3. Add 1 lb. grated swiss cheese to meat mixture.

Meats
and Meat Dishes

from
Amish and Mennonite
kitchens

Chicken Pot Pie

1 3½–4 lb. chicken   Makes 8-10 servings
1 cup celery, chopped
pinch saffron
salt and pepper to taste

1. Cook chicken and celery in 2 quarts of water until chicken is tender.
2. Remove meat from bones and set aside.
3. Add water to broth to make 3½ quarts, (several chicken bouillon cubes may be added to strengthen the broth).
4. Bring broth to boil. Drop pot pie squares into boiling broth and cook until tender. Return chicken to broth. Serve piping hot.

Pot Pie Dough

5 eggs
½ cup water
2¾ – 3¼ cups flour

1. Combine eggs and water and beat well.
2. Gradually add flour until soft dough is formed.
3. Cut into 3 parts. Roll each part on a cloth, rolling as thin as possible, using an additional 1 cup of flour to flour cloth

and dough so it handles well.
4. Cut into 1 inch squares with pastry wheel and drop into boiling broth.

Variation:
   Add 5 sliced, cooked potatoes to pot pie.

Creamed Chicken

2 Tbsp. butter or   Makes 4-6 servings
   chicken fat
2 Tbsp. flour
½ tsp. salt
dash of pepper
1 tsp. minced celery leaves
1 cup milk
1 cup chicken broth
2 cups cooked, diced chicken

1. Melt butter. Add flour, salt, pepper, and celery leaves. Stir until smooth.
2. Add milk and chicken broth. Bring to a boil and boil 5 minutes, stirring constantly.
3. Add chicken and heat thoroughly.
4. Serve with floating islands.

from
Amish and Mennonite
kitchens

Floating Islands

4 cups flour
5 egg yolks
12 Tbsp. margarine or butter
milk

1. Cut together flour, egg yolks, and margarine to form coarse crumbs.
2. Add milk enough to moisten so dough can be rolled.
3. Roll dough thinly on floured surface. Cut into 1" squares or diamond shapes. Place on cookie sheet and bake at 350° until browned. You will need to watch these closely as some will finish baking before other.
4. Place islands in serving dish and cover with chunky chicken pieces and creamy broth.

Creamed chicken may also be served over hot biscuits or waffles.

Chicken Croquettes

2 cups cooked chicken,   Makes 4 servings
    ground or chopped fine
pinch of celery salt
1 tsp. lemon juice
1/8 tsp. paprika
1 Tbsp. parsley
1/4 tsp. chopped onion
1 cup white sauce

White Sauce

1 Tbsp. butter or margarine
1 Tbsp. flour
1/2 tsp. salt
1/8 tsp. pepper
1 cup milk

1. Melt butter; then add flour, salt, and pepper and mix well. Gradually add milk, stirring constantly until thickened.
2. Combine chicken, seasonings, and white sauce. Shape into croquettes and roll in bread crumbs. Then roll croquettes in beaten egg and again in bread crumbs.
3. Fry in deep fat for four minutes.

Meats
and Meat Dishes

from
Amish and Mennonite
kitchens

Chicken Pie

1	4 lb. chicken	Makes 4-6 servings

1 bay leaf
2 stems celery, finely chopped
1 onion, thinly sliced
3 cups potatoes, cooked and diced
2 cups carrots, cooked and diced
1 cup peas, cooked
2 Tbsp. margarine or butter
2 Tbsp. flour
1 tsp. salt
⅛ tsp. pepper
1 cup milk
2 cups chicken broth
½ tsp. worcestershire sauce

1. Cook chicken with bay leaf until chicken is tender. Discard bay leaf. Remove meat from bones. Reserve chicken broth.
2. Combine vegetables and chicken and pour into casserole.
3. Melt margarine. Stir in flour, salt, and pepper. Gradually add milk and chicken broth. Stir in worcestershire sauce. Pour over vegetable/chicken mixture.
4. Cover casserole with pie crust.
5. Bake at 425° for 35 minutes. Reduce

oven temperature to warm and allow to set for 15-20 minutes. This helps to blend the flavors.

Pie Crust
- 1 cup flour
- ½ tsp. salt
- ⅓ cup shortening
- 3 Tbsp. cold water

1. Combine flour and salt. Cut in shortening till fine crumbs are formed.
2. Add water, 1 Tbsp. at a time and toss until all particles of flour have been dampened. Work mixture into a ball. Roll out and put on top of vegetables.

"Especially good on a cold day."

Meats
and Meat Dishes

Chicken Roast

3 whole chickens
6½ quarts bread crumbs
½ lb. margarine
3 cups chopped celery
1 cup chopped onion
6 eggs beaten
½ lb. margarine, melted
2 tsp. parsley flakes
6 tsp. salt
1 tsp. celery salt
1 tsp. garlic or onion salt
1 tsp. paprika
1 tsp. pepper
3 tsp. poultry seasoning

1. Cook chickens till tender. Debone chicken and reserve broth.
2. Brown bread crumbs in ½ lb. margarine, stirring constantly.
3. Combine bread crumbs and all other ingredients except chicken. Mix well and add chicken broth till mixture is very moist.
4. Put chicken meat in bottom of a large roast pan. Cover with bread mixture.

5. Roast in a slow oven till golden brown (250° for 1½-2 hours).

"The traditional Amish wedding dish."

Baked Chicken
Dip chicken pieces in evaporated milk and then in cornflake crumbs. Arrange in single layer in roast pan or casserole. Cover. Bake at 350° for 1½ hours or at 200° while at church on Sunday morning.

Beef Roast

3-4 lb. beef roast   Makes 6 servings
2 tsp. salt
¾ tsp. pepper
¾ cup water

1. Rub meat with salt and pepper. Place roast in roasting pan.
2. Add 1 cup water. Cover and bake at 325° for 1½ hours.
3. Remove lid and bake an additional ½ hour to allow meat to brown.

Beef Gravy

3 cups water
2 Tbsp. flour
1 cup water
salt and pepper to taste

1. Add 3 cups water to browned beef drippings. Bring mixture to boil on top of the stove.
2. Make a smooth paste with the flour and 1 cup water.
3. Add paste to boiling drippings and water in a thin stream. Stir quickly and

constantly to prevent lumps. Add seasonings. Heat until thickened.

4. Serve with sliced beef roast and mashed potatoes.

Poor Man's Steak

2 lbs. ground beef   Makes 4 servings
1 cup cracker crumbs
1 cup milk
1 tsp. salt
¼ tsp. pepper
1 onion, chopped

1. Mix all ingredients together. Pat mixture out to ½" thickness on paper lined cookie sheets. Cover and refrigerate overnight.

2. Cut meat into serving size pieces. Coat with flour. Brown pieces in small amount of hot fat. Place in roasting pan and cover with mushroom sauce mixed with 1¼ cup water.

3. Bake, covered, at 300° for 1½ hours.

Mushroom Sauce

3 Tbsp. margarine
¼ cup mushrooms, chopped
1 Tbsp. minced onion
3 Tbsp. flour
¼ tsp. salt
dash pepper
1 cup milk

1. Melt margarine. Add mushrooms and onion and sauté till tender. Add flour, salt, and pepper and stir until bubbly.
2. Gradually add milk, stirring constantly. Cook and stir until thickened.

Meat Loaf

1 egg   *Makes 4-6 servings*
¾ cup quick oats or bread crumbs
1 cup tomato juice
½ onion, minced
1 Tbsp. soy sauce
1 tsp. salt
¼ tsp. pepper
1½ lb. ground beef

1. Beat egg. Add remaining ingredients and mix well. Form into a loaf and bake at 350° for 1 hour.

Variation:
   Baked meat loaf may be placed on oven proof platter and frosted with mashed potatoes. Return to oven until potatoes are golden brown.

Sauce for Meat Loaf or Ham Loaf
   2 Tbsp. honey
   1 Tbsp. catsup
   1 tsp. lemon juice

   Combine and use to baste meat loaf or ham loaf.

"A nice moist loaf that stays together."

Meats
and Meat Dishes

from
Amish and Mennonite
kitchens

Baked Pork and Sauerkraut

1 pork roast   Makes 4 to 6 servings
27 oz. sauerkraut
3 cups water

1. Place pork roast in center of roast pan. Arrange sauerkraut around meat. Pour water over all.
2. Bake, covered, at 325° for 2½-3 hours, depending on the size of the pork roast. Add more water if sauerkraut dries during baking.

This is a delicious cold weather dish. Serve it straight from the roast pan with mounds of mashed potatoes and home canned applesauce.

Baked Pork Chops

Place 6 pork chops in bottom of shallow baking dish. Sprinkle with salt. Bake at 350° for 15 minutes. Cover each chop with bread filling and place 2-3 Tbsp. apple-sauce on top of filling. Return to oven and bake 1 hour longer.

Scrapple

1 lb. pork pudding meat
1 qt. water or pork broth
salt and pepper to taste
1½ cups corn meal
¼ cup buckwheat flour

Makes 3~4 lbs.
of scrapple

1. Stir pudding meat into 1 quart seasoned rapidly boiling water or pork broth.
2. When the mixture reaches the boiling point slowly add the corn meal and buckwheat flour. Stir constantly until thickened.
3. Cover and let simmer for 15 minutes over low heat.
4. Pour into two 1-lb. loaf pans. Cool thoroughly; then refrigerate promptly.
5. When scrapple is set, cut in ⅜ to ½ inch slices and fry in hot, greased skillet. When slices are browned and crusty, turn and brown on other side.
6. Serve hot with catsup, syrup, or apple butter.

"A hearty and traditional breakfast dish!"

Meats
and Meat Dishes

from
Amish and Mennonite
kitchens

Pig Stomach

1 large, well cleaned   Makes 4 servings
   pig stomach
1½ lbs. bulk sausage meat
6 medium potatoes, peeled and diced
1 small onion, chopped

1.   Cook potatoes and onion together until potatoes are tender. Separate sausage meat into small pieces and add to potato mixture. Stir and cook only until sausage loses its reddish color.

2.   Drain off excess liquid. Stuff mixture loosely into stomach and close all openings with skewers laced with string. Place in roast pan with ½ cup water. Place remaining mixture that will not fit in stomach in a buttered casserole.

3.   Cover roast pan containing the stomach and bake at 350° for 2-2½ hours. After first hour prick stomach with sharp fork. Place casserole of remaining mixture in oven, uncovered and bake only for the last 40-45 minutes of baking time.

Overstuffing the stomach may cause it to burst while baking because the stomach shrinks considerably.

Variations:
1. Mix sweet potatoes with white potatoes.
2. Add 2 cups uncooked lima beans to stuffing.
3. Add 1 cup chopped carrots to stuffing.
4. Add 1 stalk chopped celery to stuffing.
5. Add ½ loaf of cubed bread to stuffing.
6. Add 1½-2 cups chopped cabbage to stuffing.

"We always called it 'Hog Maul'. We like to eat it at special times – Christmas or New Years or birthdays."

Meats
and Meat Dishes

Sweet and Sour Sausage Balls

1 lb. sausage meat   Makes 5-6 servings
1/2 cup bread crumbs or cracker crumbs
1 egg, slightly beaten

Mix together. Form into small balls and brown.

Sauce
    3/4 cup catsup
    1/8 cup white vinegar
    1/8 cup soy sauce
    1/4 cup brown sugar

1. Mix together. Pour over browned sausage balls and simmer for 30 minutes.
2. Add water as needed during simmering to keep mixture from getting too dry.
3. Serve with rice or noodles.

"It's a lively way to serve sausage. The sweet and sour flavor is a favorite of ours!"

Barbecued Meat Balls

1 lb. ground beef   Makes 6 meatballs
1 egg
1 cup cracker crumbs
1 tsp. salt
¼ tsp. pepper
1 Tbsp. finely chopped onion
3 Tbsp. brown sugar
¼ cup catsup
⅛ tsp. nutmeg
1 tsp. dry mustard

1. Combine meat, egg, ¾ cup crumbs, salt, pepper, and onion. Mix well.
2. Mix together sugar, catsup, nutmeg, and mustard. Add half of this sauce to meat mixture. Mix well. Shape meat mixture into 6 balls and place in 3" muffin cups. Top balls with remaining sauce. Sprinkle with remaing crumbs.
3. Bake at 400° for 30 minutes.

"Very good. I will add this to my list of favorites for quick preparation and short baking time."

Meats
and Meat Dishes

from
Amish and Mennonite
kitchens

Barbecued Hamburger

2 lb. hamburger   *Makes 8 servings*
2 onions, chopped finely
½ cup catsup
1 cup tomato juice
6 Tbsp. brown sugar
6 Tbsp. apple cider vinegar
6 tsp. worcestershire sauce
6 tsp. prepared mustard

1. Brown hamburger and onion together.
2. Add remaining ingredients and simmer slowly for 45 minutes.
3. Pile into hamburger rolls to serve.

Turkey Barbecue

¼ cup butter or   *Makes 6-8 servings*
   margarine
½ cup onion, chopped
1 cup celery, chopped
¼ cup green pepper, chopped
¾ cup catsup
1 tsp. salt
2 Tbsp. brown sugar
1½ tsp. chili powder

1 Tbsp. worcestershire sauce
dash pepper
4 cups chopped, cooked turkey

1. Cook onion, celery, and pepper in butter until soft.
2. Add remaining ingredients except turkey and cook 5 minutes.
3. Add turkey. Heat thoroughly.

Tuna Burgers

1 7 oz. can tuna fish   Makes 6 sandwiches
1 small onion, minced
¼ cup mayonaise
½ cup diced or grated cheese
1 cup chopped celery
6 hamburger rolls

1. Combine all ingredients for filling. Salt and pepper to taste.
2. Butter inside of rolls. Fill rolls and wrap in foil.
3. Bake at 350° for 20 minutes.

from
Amish and Mennonite
kitchens

Fried Oysters

12 large oysters   *Makes 12 oysters*
2 eggs
2 Tbsp. milk
1-1½ cup cracker crumbs

1. Beat eggs and milk lightly.
2. Dip oysters first in egg mixture and then into cracker crumbs. Repeat this process once or twice to coat oysters.
3. Fry in deep fat until golden brown.

Scalloped Oysters

4 cups crackers,   *Makes 4 to 5 servings*
   coarsely crushed
1 10 oz. can medium sized oysters
2 cups milk
1 egg
1 tsp. salt
pepper to taste
⅓ cup butter or margarine

1. Line 1½ quart casserole with half of the crackers. Place half of the oysters on crushed crackers. Layer remaining crackers on top of oysters followed by the rest of the oysters.

2. Beat egg and add milk, salt, and pepper to it.

3. Just before baking pour mixture over oysters and crackers. Arrange butter in thin slices on top.

4. Bake at 375° for 30 minutes.

Deviled Clams

   1 dozen large clams   Makes 12 clams
   ½ cup cold water
   3 hard boiled eggs, chopped
   onion and parsley to taste
   bread crumbs
   salt and pepper

1. Scrub clams well. Steam open. Save clam shells.

2. Grind clams. Add water, eggs, onion, and parsley. Thicken mixture with bread crumbs and season with salt and pepper. Form balls and pack mixture into half of the clam shells. Gently lower filled shell into hot oil and fry until golden brown. Clams may be fried ahead of time and kept warm in the oven.

from
Amish and Mennonite
kitchens

Salmon Croquettes

2 cups flaked salmon   Makes 8 croquettes
4 Tbsp. flour
1 egg
2 Tbsp. minced onion
1 tsp. salt
1 cup bread crumbs
½ cup milk

1. Combine all ingredients and mix well.
2. Fry in hot oil in heavy skillet till browned on both sides.

Beef Tongue

1 fresh beef tongue
⅔ cup salt
⅓ cup brown sugar
pinch pepper

1. Mix salt, sugar, and pepper. Rub salt mixture into tongue. Place in airtight container in cool place for 3 days. Turn daily.

2. On the 4th day remove and rinse well. Cook about 2 hours or until tender. Cool 10 minutes. Peel outer skin from tongue.
3. Cool and slice.

Sour Gravy

2 cups cooked, cut-up roast beef
2 cups water
⅓ cup sugar
2 Tbsp. vinegar
3 Tbsp. flour

Makes 2-4 servings

1. Combine beef, water, sugar, and vinegar. Bring mixture to a boil.
2. Mix flour with enough water to make a smooth, thin paste. Gradually stir into beef mixture and cook until thickened.

"Delicious served on fried mush, stewed crackers, or old-fashioned baked egg omelet."

Liver Patties

1 lb. liver
2 slices bacon
1 small onion
1 egg, beaten
2 Tbsp. flour
1 tsp. salt
1/8 tsp. pepper

Makes 20 2½" patties

1. Grind liver, bacon, and onion in meat grinder or chop very fine.
2. Add beaten egg, flour, salt, and pepper and mix well.
3. Drop mixture by spoonfuls onto greased griddle or skillet.
4. Fry just a few minutes on each side.

"Left over patties make good sandwiches."

Barbecued Liver

Makes 4 servings

½ cup tomato juice
¼ cup water
2 Tbsp. apple cider vinegar
2 Tbsp. catsup
1 Tbsp. worcestershire sauce
1 Tbsp. brown sugar
½ tsp. salt
½ tsp. dry mustard
⅛ tsp. chili powder
2 Tbsp. bacon drippings
1 lb. beef liver

1. Combine first nine ingredients in small saucepan. Simmer for 15 minutes, stirring occasionally
2. Remove any veins or skin from liver. Cut into ½ inch strips.
3. Heat bacon drippings in large skillet. Add liver strips, stirring constantly over high heat, just until the meat looses its red color. Overcooking liver makes it tough.
4. Stir the barbecue sauce into the skillet containing the liver. Simmer together only until piping hot.
5. Serve over rice or noodles.

Meats
and Meat Dishes

from
Amish and Mennonite
kitchens

Creamed Dried Beef

4 Tbsp. butter   Makes 4 servings
¼ lb. dried beef, thinly sliced
½ cup water
4 Tbsp. flour
2½ cups milk

1. Brown butter in heavy skillet. Add shredded pieces of dried beef. Brown slightly. Add water and boil until water is evaporated. This helps to make the beef tender.
2. Sprinkle flour over beef and allow to brown slightly.
3. Slowly add milk and cook over low heat, stirring constantly. Cook until smooth and thickened.
4. Serve over baked potatoes or toast.

"A quickie meal – and substantial. The meat is so flavorful you only need a little bit to serve a bunch!"

Snitz and Knepp

1 ham hock   Makes about 4 servings
1½ cups dried apples
2 Tbsp. brown sugar

1. Place ham hock in heavy saucepan. Cover with 2 quarts of water and boil 2 hours.
2. Add apples and brown sugar. Add an additional 1½ quarts of water and cook until apples are soft. Add knepp.

Knepp

2 cups flour
3 tsp. baking powder
½ tsp. salt
1 egg, beaten
2 Tbsp. melted butter
⅓-½ cup milk

1. Mix flour, baking powder, and salt. Add beaten egg, butter, and milk. Use only enough milk to make a sticky dough that will drop easily off a spoon.
2. Drop by spoonfuls into boiling ham and apple mixture. Cover tightly and boil for 15 minutes. Do not peek.

Meats
and Meat Dishes

Casseroles

from
Amish and Mennonite
kitchens

from
Amish and Mennonite
kitchens

Casseroles

Casseroles are wonderful inventions. They can be designed to fit any schedule and taste preference; they can take on the personality of whatever is ripe in the garden, plentiful in the refrigerator, or on special at the store! And what's more efficient than a one-main-dish meal?

We suspect that casseroles were first created in the kitchens of conscientious cooks who came up on suppertime, having no chance to make the roast or mash the potatoes.

Some spontaneous combinations became traditions. All the eat-ers around the table agreed they worked. Then the concoctions were either written down or practiced so often they weren't forgotten. Those are the recipes we offer here. Sturdy and basic. Now and then a surprise. Economical. But satisfyingly filling.

Dairyland Casserole

8 oz. noodles   Makes 10-12 servings
1½ lb. ground beef
2 cups tomato sauce
⅛ tsp. worchestershire sauce
⅓ cup onion, chopped
1 Tbsp. green pepper, chopped
8 oz. cream cheese
1 cup cottage cheese
½ cup sour cream
3 Tbsp. melted butter

1. Cook noodles until tender. Drain and set aside.
2. Brown beef. Add tomato sauce, worchestershire sauce, onion, and pepper.
3. Combine cheeses and sour cream.
4. Butter large casserole. Pour in half of the noodles. Add cheese and cream mixture and cover with remaining noodles. Top with beef mixture. Drizzle melted butter over top. Bake at 350° for 30-45 minutes.

Crunchy Hot Chicken Casserole

3 Tbsp. butter   Makes 8 servings
¼ cup mushrooms, chopped
1 Tbsp. onion, chopped
3 Tbsp. flour
1 cup milk
1 cup celery, chopped
¾ cup mayonnaise
2 tsp. lemon juice
¾ tsp. salt
3 hard-boiled eggs, chopped
3 cups rice, cooked
2 chicken breasts, cooked and cubed
butter and Rice Krispies

1. Melt 3 Tbsp. butter. Sauté mushrooms and onion until tender. Add flour and stir until smooth. Gradually add milk and stir until thickened.
2. Combine sauce with all remaining ingredients except butter and Rice Krispies. Mix well.
3. Turn into a buttered baking dish. Sprinkle casserole with Rice Krispies. Dot with butter. Bake at 375° for 30 minutes.

Baked Chicken and Rice

½ cup plus 1 Tbsp.   Makes 6-8 servings
  butter or margarine, melted
½ cup mushrooms, chopped
¼ cup celery, chopped
½ cup plus 1 Tbsp. flour
1 Tbsp. salt
¼ tsp. pepper
4½ cups milk
1⅓ cups water
1 cup long grain rice, uncooked
dash of garlic salt
6-8 seasoned chicken parts

1. Add mushrooms and celery to melted butter in saucepan and sauté until golden. Stir in flour and seasonings. Gradually add milk and bring to the boiling point, stirring constantly until thickened. Remove from heat.
2. Blend in water. Add rice and garlic salt, mixing well.
3. Pour into large roaster or baking pan. Arrange chicken pieces on top of rice mixture.
4. Cover and bake 3 hours at 300°.

Chicken Spaghetti

1 stewing chicken Makes 12 servings
3 Tbsp. butter or margarine
6 celery stems, chopped
2 onions, chopped
¼ cup mushrooms, chopped
3 Tbsp. flour
1 cup milk
½ lb. sharp cheese, grated
1 pint chicken stock
1 Tbsp. Worcestershire sauce
salt and pepper to taste
½ lb. spaghetti
1 small bottle stuffed olives,
    chopped or sliced
1 cup pecans, chopped

1.   Cook chicken in water until tender. Remove from bones and cut in large pieces. Reserve stock.
2. Melt butter. Sauté celery, onions, and mushrooms until tender. Add flour and stir to form a smooth paste. Gradually add milk. Stir until thickened. Add cheese. Stir until melted. Add chicken stock and seasonings.
3. Cook spaghetti in water for 3 minutes.

Drain. Add to stock mixture and let stand for 1 hour. Mix in chicken and olives.

4. Pour into a 9"x 15" shallow casserole. Top with pecans. Bake at 350° for ½ hour.

Variation:
    Add 2 cups cooked peas and carrots.

Country Chicken Supper

4 oz. spaghetti,   Makes 8 servings
    uncooked
1 lb. mild cream cheese, cubed or grated
1 cup milk
½ cup mayonnaise
2 cups cooked chicken (or turkey) cubed
1½ cups peas and carrots, cooked

1. Cook spaghetti. Drain and set aside.
2. Heat cheese, milk, and mayonnaise together over low heat, stirring until sauce is smooth.
3. Add chicken, vegetables and spaghetti to sauce, mixing well. Pour into 2-quart casserole.
4. Bake at 350° for 35-40 minutes.

Chicken Broccoli Casserole

1¼ lb. fresh broccoli   Makes 10 servings
    chopped and cooked (or 2 10 oz. pkgs.),
4-6 cups cooked chicken, coarsely diced
6 Tbsp. butter or margarine
6 Tbsp. flour
2 tsp. salt
¼ tsp. pepper
3 cups milk
½ cup mayonnaise
1 tsp. lemon juice
1 cup cheddar cheese, grated
2 Tbsp. butter or margarine
½ cup bread crumbs

1. Layer broccoli on bottom of greased 9" x 13" baking dish. Layer chicken over broccoli.
2. In a saucepan melt the 6 Tbsp. butter. Stir in the flour, salt, and pepper. Gradually stir in the milk and continue stirring until the white sauce is smooth and comes to a boil. Remove from heat.
3. Combine mayonnaise and lemon juice with white sauce and pour over chicken and broccoli. Sprinkle with cheese.
4. Melt 2 Tbsp. butter. Stir in bread crumbs and sprinkle over casserole.
5. Bake at 350° for 35-40 minutes.

Chicken Macaroni Dinner

1 cup macaroni,   Makes 8 servings
   uncooked
1 Tbsp. butter or margarine
1 Tbsp. flour
1 tsp. salt
⅛ tsp. pepper
1 cup milk
½ cup chicken broth
1½ cups cooked chicken, diced
1 cup corn, fresh or frozen
2 Tbsp. butter, melted
½ cup bread crumbs

1. Cook macaroni. Drain and set aside.
2. Melt 1 Tbsp. butter. Stir in flour and seasonings. Gradually add milk and chicken broth. Bring to the boiling point, stirring constantly until thickened.
3. Mix together the macaroni, white sauce, chicken, and corn. Pour into a greased baking dish.
4. Stir bread crumbs into melted butter and sprinkle over casserole. Bake at 350° for 45 minutes.

Casseroles

Chicken Corn Pie

1 stewing chicken   Makes 6-8 servings
1 qt. corn, cooked
pastry enough for 2 double-crust pies

1.   Cook chicken and remove from bones. Make a thin gravy with the chicken stock.
2.   Line 2 9" pie plates with pastry. Place meat and corn in alternate layers in crust. Add gravy enough to barely cover chicken corn mixture. Cover with crust and seal edges. Bake at 425° for 20 minutes. Eat hot with remaining gravy.

Variations:
   1. Delete 3 cups corn. In place of corn add cooked carrots, peas, and cubed potatoes.
   2. Beef Vegetable Pie – follow above procedure but substitute 1½ lb. beef in place of chicken. Cook beef until tender. Cube and follow procedure using beef broth. Use 1 cup each peas, carrots, potatoes, and corn, cooked.

"Friday Night" Meat Pie

"When our family was growing up, I cleaned out the refrigerator every Friday evening. I gathered all the leftover vegetables and meat that had collected that week, and then cut the pork or beef or chicken into bite-sized pieces, added gravy if there was any, and stirred in all the leftover vegetables.

"If I didn't have many vegetables I diced a potato or two, added a little celery and onion, cooked them until they were soft and put them in the mixture. I also liked to add some herb seasoning.

"Then I poured it into a casserole, and dropped biscuit batter on top. I baked it, then, at 425° for 12-15 minutes.

"It's a delicious way to get rid of left-overs. Our family loved it.

"Another tip for using leftover vegetables is to keep a box in the freezing unit of the refrigerator. Then add layer upon layer of corn, peas, beans — whatever — to use in soup. The vegetables won't have a stale taste!"

Casseroles

from
Amish and Mennonite
kitchens

Lazy Day Stew

Makes 8 servings

2 lb. beef cubes
2 cups carrots, sliced
2 cups potatoes, diced
2 medium onions, sliced
1 cup celery, chopped
1½ cups green beans
2 tsp. quick cooking tapioca
1 Tbsp. salt
½ tsp. pepper
1 8 oz. can tomato sauce
1 cup water
1 Tbsp. brown sugar

1. Place raw beef cubes (do not brown) in a single layer in a 2½ quart casserole or roast pan.
2. Add vegetables and/or any others you desire.
3. Sprinkle tapioca, salt, and pepper over top. Pour tomato sauce mixed with water over vegetables and seasonings.
4. Crumble brown sugar over all.
5. Cover tightly and do not peep! Bake at 325° for 3 hours.

Variation:
    Stew may be made in a slow cooker.

Sausage and Apple Casserole

1½ lb. link sausage   Makes 8 servings
    cut in small pieces, or
    1½ lb. bulk sausage in small balls
4 medium apples, pared and sliced
3 medium sweet potatoes, pared and
    sliced
½ tsp. salt
1 Tbsp. flour
2 Tbsp. sugar

1. Fry sausage, saving drippings.
2. Combine salt, flour, and sugar. Arrange sausage, apples, and potatoes in layers in a casserole. Sprinkle some flour mixture over each layer. Top with a layer of sausage. Sprinkle casserole with 1 Tbsp. sausage drippings. Cover tightly. Bake at 375° for 1 hour.

Casseroles

Six Layer Sausage Casserole

1 lb. pork sausage   Makes 6 servings
(loose)
1½ cups raw potatoes, sliced
1 cup raw onions, sliced
1 cup raw carrots, sliced
½ cup rice, uncooked
1½ cups canned tomatoes, including juice
1 tsp. salt
⅛ tsp. pepper
2 Tbsp. sugar

1. Brown sausage in heavy skillet. Drain off excess fat.
2. Place sausage in bottom of a 2 quart casserole. Cover with layers of potatoes, onions, carrots, and rice. Add tomatoes with juice.
3. Combine salt, pepper, and sugar. Sprinkle over top. Bake, covered at 350° for 1½ hours.

Truckpatch Dinner

bacon slices
ground beef
potatoes
peas
carrots
salt and pepper to taste

1. Arrange a layer of bacon on bottom of roast pan or casserole. Add a layer of raw hamburger. Add a layer of sliced potatoes, seasoned with salt and pepper. Bake at 375° for 1 hour.
2. Remove from oven and add a layer of peas and carrots. Return to oven and bake 45-60 minutes longer.

Variation:
Pour 1½ cups tomatoes over all before baking.

Casseroles

Vegetable Cheese Casserole

4 cups broccoli   Makes 6-8 servings
2 cups ham, cooked and diced
2 Tbsp. butter or margarine
2 Tbsp. flour
½ tsp. salt
1½ cups milk
¼ cup cheese, grated or cut fine
paprika
3 slices bread, buttered

1. Cook broccoli in salt water, just until tender. Put into buttered baking dish. Sprinkle ham over vegetables.
2. Melt butter. Stir in flour and salt. Gradually add milk, stirring constantly until the white sauce thickens and comes to a boiling point. Then pour over broccoli and ham.
3. Sprinkle cheese and paprika over top.
4. Cut bread in cubes and arrange on top of casserole.
5. Bake at 375° for 15-20 minutes.

Mother's Tomato Rice Meat Pie

1 lb. ground beef   Makes 12 servings
¼ cup green pepper, chopped
1 small onion, chopped
½ cup dry bread crumbs
salt and pepper to taste
2 cups tomato sauce
1⅓ cups minute rice
1 cup water
1 cup cheddar cheese, grated

1. Combine beef, pepper, onion, bread crumbs, salt, pepper, and ½ cup tomato sauce. Mix well. Pat into bottom and sides of a greased 9" square pan.
2. Combine remaining tomato sauce, rice, water, and ½ cup cheese. Spoon mixture into meat shell. Cover and bake at 350° for 25 minutes. Top with remaining cheese. Bake, uncovered 10-15 minutes longer.

Casseroles

Stuffed Cabbage

1 head cabbage   Makes 8~10 servings
    with large loose leaves
1 onion, minced
1 lb. ground beef
1 cup rice, cooked
1 egg, beaten
salt and pepper to taste
¼ cup tomato paste
½ cup water
1 cup cultured sour cream

1. Remove large outer leaves (8~10) from cabbage and cook in boiling salt water for 3 minutes. Drain.
2. Brown hamburger and onion together. Stir in cooked rice, egg, salt and pepper.
3. Place hamburger rice mixture on cabbage leaves. Roll up and fasten with toothpicks. Place in greased baking dish.
4. Stir together tomato paste, water, and sour cream. Then pour over cabbage rolls.
5. Cover and bake at 350° for 1 hour.

Cabbage Hamburger Bake

1 head cabbage   Makes 6~8 servings
1 lb. hamburger
3 Tbsp. butter or margarine
3 Tbsp. flour
1 tsp. salt
dash of pepper
1½ cups milk
1 tsp. parsley flakes
2 Tbsp. butter or margarine
½ cup bread crumbs

1. Slice cabbage; then steam until wilted. Spoon into greased casserole dish.
2. Brown hamburger lightly. Pour over wilted cabbage in baking dish.
3. Melt the 3 Tbsp. butter. Stir in the flour, salt, and pepper. Gradually stir in the milk and continue stirring until the white sauce is smooth and comes to a boil. Stir in the parsley flakes; then pour the sauce over the cabbage and hamburger.
4. Melt the 2 Tbsp butter. Stir in bread crumbs. Crumble over white sauce.
5. Bake at 350° for 30 minutes.

Casseroles

Beef, Corn, and Noodles

1 lb. hamburger,   Makes 8 servings
   browned
1 pt. corn, cooked
2 cups noodles, cooked
2 cups beef broth
1 Tbsp. butter
3 hard-boiled eggs, diced

1. Mix together the hamburger, corn, noodles, and broth. Pour into greased baking dish.
2. Dot with butter. Sprinkle egg over top.
3. Bake at 350° for 40~45 minutes.

Cheese Soufflé

2 Tbsp. butter   Makes 2 servings
3 Tbsp. flour
½ cup milk
½ cup cheese, grated
2 large or 3 small eggs, separated
½ tsp. salt

1. Melt butter. Add flour and stir to make a smooth paste. Gradually add milk. Stir until thickened. Add cheese. Stir until melted. Add egg yolks and salt.
2. Beat egg whites until stiff. Gently fold into sauce. Turn into greased casserole or soufflé dish. Bake at 325° for 25 minutes.

Baked Carrots and Apples

4 cups carrots,   Makes 7 servings
   cut in ½" pieces
3 cups apples, peeled, cored, and sliced
¼ cup honey
2 Tbsp. butter or margarine
paprika

1. Steam carrots until tender. Drain. Stir in apples and honey.
2. Turn into buttered casserole. Dot with butter. Cover and bake at 350° for 50 minutes.
3. Stir. Sprinkle with paprika. Bake, uncovered, an additional 10 minutes.

Carrot Casserole

½ cup butter   Makes 12-16 servings
1 small onion, chopped
¼ cup flour
1 tsp. salt
¼ tsp. pepper
½ tsp. dry mustard
¼ tsp. celery salt
2 cups milk
½ lb. cheese, sliced
12 large carrots, thinly sliced, cooked
buttered bread crumbs

1. Melt butter. Add onion, flour, and seasonings and stir until smooth. Gradually add milk. Stir over medium heat until thickened.
2. Arrange half of carrots in bottom of a 2½ qt. casserole. Add cheese slices. Top with remaining carrots. Pour sauce over all. Top with buttered bread crumbs. Bake at 375° for 30 minutes.

Scalloped Potatoes

6 medium potatoes
    cooked in jackets
½ cup butter
1 tsp. parsley flakes
¼ cup onion, chopped
1 tsp. dry or prepared mustard
¼ tsp. pepper
1 tsp. salt
¼ cup milk
¼ cup cheese, grated

Makes 12 servings

1. Dice potatoes and place in greased casserole.
2. Melt butter. Add other ingredients and cook until cheese is melted. Pour sauce over potatoes and bake at 350° for 45 minutes.

Variation:
    Omit cheese. Add 1 cup sour cream plus 1 lb. cooked, diced ham.

Casseroles

Green Beans and Potato Casserole

1½ cups cooked green beans   Makes 6 servings
1 cup potatoes, cooked and diced
½ cup celery, diced
4 slices bacon
1 small onion, chopped
1½ Tbsp. flour
1 cup undiluted evaporated milk
1 cup cheese, shredded
⅓ cup cracker crumbs

1. Combine beans, potatoes, and celery. Place in greased 1 quart casserole.
2. Fry bacon until crisp. Drain, saving 1 Tbsp. drippings. Crumble bacon and set aside. Sauté onion in drippings.
3. Add flour and stir to a smooth paste. Slowly add milk. Cook, stirring constantly until thickened. Add cheese. Stir until melted. Pour over vegetables in casserole and stir well.
4. Sprinkle with cracker crumbs. Add crumbled bacon on top. Bake at 350° for 30 minutes.

Zucchini Casserole

1 lb. ground   Makes 6-8 servings
    beef, browned
1½ lb. zucchini, cooked and sliced
1½ cups potatoes, cooked and cubed
½ cup cheddar cheese, shredded
salt and pepper to taste
3 Tbsp. butter
1 Tbsp. onion, minced
¼ cup mushrooms, chopped
3 Tbsp. flour
1¼ cups milk
1 cup soft bread crumbs mixed with
    2 Tbsp. melted butter

1. In buttered casserole arrange layers of beef, zucchini, potatoes, and cheese. Season to taste.
2. Melt butter. Sauté onion and mushrooms until tender. Add flour. Stir until smooth. Gradually add milk and stir until thickened. Pour sauce over layered ingredients in casserole. Top with crumbs. Bake at 350° for 1 hour.

Zucchini Scallop

Makes 10 servings

2 cups zucchini, cooked
2 cups saltine crackers, crumbled
2 Tbsp. onion, minced
1 cup cheese, cubed
1 cup milk
1 egg, beaten
2 Tbsp. butter, melted
pepper

1. Layer zucchini, crackers, onion, and cheese in a 2 qt. greased casserole. Combine milk and egg. Pour over zucchini mixture. Pour butter over all. Sprinkle with pepper.
2. Bake at 350° for 45 minutes.

Tuna Noodle Casserole

1 8 oz. pkg. noodles   Makes 24 servings
8 Tbsp. butter
5 Tbsp. flour
2½ cups milk
1 8 oz. pkg. cream cheese
1 large can tuna
salt and pepper to taste
6 oz. mild cheese, sliced
1½ cups soft bread crumbs

1. Cook noodles in water until tender. Drain and set aside.
2. Melt 5 Tbsp. of the butter. Add flour and stir to form a smooth paste. Gradually add milk and stir until thickened. Add cream cheese and tuna. Stir until cheese is melted. Add seasonings.
3. In greased casserole, layer noodles, sauce, and sliced cheese alternately.
4. Melt remaining butter. Stir in bread crumbs. Sprinkle buttered crumbs over top of casserole. Bake at 350° for 30 minutes.

Variations:
1. Use salmon in place of tuna.
2. Add 1 cup peas and 2 chopped eggs.

Easy Tuna Fondue

5 slices bread   Makes 10-12 servings
½ cup cheese
1 12 oz. can tuna
2 cups milk
3 eggs, slightly beaten
½ tsp. onion, grated
paprika or parsley flakes

1. Cut bread in ½" cubes. Spread half in bottom of greased 2 qt. casserole. Sprinkle with half of cheese. Add tuna. Cover with remaining bread and cheese.
2. Combine milk, eggs, salt, and onion. Pour over mixture. Sprinkle top with paprika or parsley. Bake at 325° for 50 minutes.

Egg Strata

waffles   Makes 6-8 servings

1 lb. ham,
     cooked and ground
½ lb. cheddar cheese, grated
2 Tbsp. butter
6 eggs
3 cups milk
½ tsp. salt
¼ tsp. pepper

1. Place a single layer of waffles in bottom of a 9"x 13" baking dish. Cover with ground ham. Sprinkle half of the cheese over ham. Cover with a second layer of waffles and the remaining cheese. Dot with butter.
2. Combine eggs, milk, and seasonings. Pour over waffles. Refrigerate 4 hours or overnight. Bake at 350° for 40 minutes. Remove from oven and allow to stand 10 or 15 minutes before serving.

Casseroles

Macaroni and Cheese

1½ cups milk,   Makes 6-8 servings
    scalded
2 cups soft bread crumbs or cubes
    (whole wheat or white)
¼ cup butter or margarine, melted
1 Tbsp. onion, chopped
1½ cups mild cheese, grated or cubed
½ tsp. salt
3 eggs, separated
1½ cups macaroni, cooked
paprika

1. Pour scalded milk over bread crumbs. Stir in butter, onion, cheese, and salt. Mix well.
2. Beat egg yolks and add. Stir in cooked macaroni.
3. Beat egg whites to form soft peaks. Fold into macaroni mixture.
4. Pour into a buttered casserole and sprinkle with paprika. Bake at 350° for 1 hour.

Macaroni Dried Beef Casserole

3 Tbsp. butter   Makes 8 servings
2 Tbsp. onion, minced
¼ cup mushrooms, chopped
3 Tbsp. flour
2½ cups milk
1 cup uncooked macaroni
1 cup cheese, cubed
2 hard boiled eggs, chopped
¼ lb. dried beef, chipped

1. Melt butter. Sauté onion and mushrooms until tender. Add flour and stir until smooth. Gradually add 1 cup of milk and stir until thickened. Remove from heat and stir in remaining milk.
2. Combine all other ingredients. Pour milk mixture over all. Mix well. Turn into greased casserole. Let stand 3-4 hours or overnight. Bake at 350° for 1 hour.

Pies

C. HAISEY '82

from
Amish and Mennonite
kitchens

Pies

There's no better dessert. You won't find a tastier bedtime or after school snack. Or so we've learned.

Pie belongs to Pennsylvania Dutch cooking like warm scrapple fits with a winter breakfast.

Pie baking traditionally happens at least once a week. And so the recipes and how-to secrets pass from mother to daughter.

Experienced pie makers create their crusts by "feel." They know their choicest fillings by memory. We've put some tried and true favorites on paper and asked some old hands to test them. Here, then, are family specialties for all to share. Enjoy!

Dutch Pear Pie

¼ cup flour   Makes 1 9" pie
¾ cup sugar
1 cup cream or canned evaporated milk
1 Tbsp. lemon juice
5 fresh pears, peeled and diced or canned
    pears in light syrup
¼ tsp. cinnamon
1 Tbsp. sugar
1 9" unbaked pie shell

1. Sift together flour and sugar. Stir in cream and lemon juice. Mix until smooth. Add pears. Pour into an unbaked pie shell. Sprinkle top with sugar and cinnamon.
2. Bake at 400° for 45-50 minutes. Cool until set.

    Apple's or peaches may be used instead of pears for an equally tasty pie.

from
Amish and Mennonite
kitchens

Apple Pie

6 cups apples,
   peeled and sliced
¾ cup sugar
¼ cup flour
1 tsp. cinnamon
3 Tbsp. water
1 9" unbaked pie shell

Makes 1 9" pie

1. Pour peeled and sliced apples into unbaked pie shell.
2. Combine sugar, flour, cinnamon, and water. Stir until smooth. Pour over apples.
3. Cover with top crust. Seal edges.
4. Bake at 375° for 1 hour.

Variations:

1. Stir apples into sugar, flour, and cinnamon mixture. Pour into pie shell and sprinkle with water. Cover with crumb topping made by mixing ½ cup butter or margarine, ½ cup brown sugar, and 1 cup flour.

2. Delete cinnamon. Add 1½ tsp. grated orange peel and ¼ cup quick cooking tapioca. In place of 1 cup apples use 1 cup cranberries.

3. Stir apples into sugar, flour, and cinnamon mixture. Pour into pie shell and sprinkle with water. Cover with coconut streusel topping made by mixing ⅓ cup brown sugar, ⅓ cup graham cracker crumbs, ¼ cup softened butter, and ½ cup flaked coconut.

Dried Snitz Pie

3 cups dried apples	Makes 1 9" pie
2¼ cups warm water	
1 tsp. lemon extract	
⅔ cup brown sugar	
1 double crust 9" unbaked pie shell	

1. Soak apples in the warm water. Cook over low heat until soft.
2. Mash apples and add lemon and sugar.
3. Pour into unbaked pie shell. Cover with top crust. Seal edges.
4. Bake at 425° for 15 minutes; then at 350° for 30 minutes. Serve warm.

from
*Amish and Mennonite
kitchens*

Sour Cream Apple Pie

Makes 1 9" pie

2 Tbsp. flour
½ cup sugar
¼ tsp salt
2½ cups chopped, pared apples
1 cup sour cream
1 egg
1½ tsp. vanilla
1 9" unbaked pie shell

1. Combine flour, sugar, and salt. Mix with apples. Pour into unbaked pie shell.
2. Beat together sour cream, egg, and vanilla. Pour over apple mixture.
3. Bake at 425° for 15 minutes and then at 350° for 30 minutes. Remove from oven and sprinkle with crumb mixture. Bake 10 minutes more at 400°.

Crumbs:

⅓ cup flour
⅓ cup sugar
1½ tsp. cinnamon
¼ cup butter

Combine all ingredients and mix to form fine crumbs.

Sour Cherry Pie

1¼ cups cherry juice   Makes 1 9" pie
1½ cups water
⅛ tsp. salt
¾ cup sugar
5½ Tbsp. tapioca
¼ tsp. almond extract
3 cups canned sour cherries, drained
1 9" unbaked pie shell

1. Heat cherry juice and 1 cup water.
2. Mix tapioca, sugar, and salt with ½ cup water until smooth. Stir slowly into hot juice and water, stirring and cooking until thickened.
3. Add almond extract. Remove from heat. Add cherries. Chill until cold. Pour into unbaked 9" pie shell. Top with pastry strips to form lattice or bake without and top with crumbs when pie is partly finished.
4. Bake at 400° on lowest oven shelf for 10-15 minutes; then turn oven to 350° and bake until finished (lower heat if pie gets too brown).

Variation:
Substitute 2 rounded Tbsp. of strawberry Danish Dessert and 3½ Tbsp. clear-jell for 5½ Tbsp. tapioca.

from
Amish and Mennonite
kitchens

Pumpkin Pie

1½ cup mashed pumpkin   Makes 1 9" pie
   or butternut squash
1 egg
½ cup milk, heated
½ cup cream, heated
1 Tbsp. flour
1 Tbsp. molasses or King Syrup
¾ cup sugar
1 tsp. cinnamon
dash of nutmeg
1 Tbsp. browned butter
pinch of salt
1 9" unbaked pie shell

1. Combine all ingredients. Pour into unbaked pie shell. Sprinkle additional cinnamon and nutmeg over top of pie.

2. Bake at 450° for 15 minutes; then at 350° for 45 minutes.

Variation:
   Add ½ cup coconut to pie mixture or sprinkle coconut in bottom of pie shell before filling, or on top of filled pie before baking.

Blueberry Pie

2¾ cups blueberries   Makes 1 9" pie
juice from berries plus water to make
    ½ cup liquid
½ cup sugar
3 Tbsp. tapioca
1 9" unbaked pie crust

1. Combine blueberries, liquid, sugar, and tapioca. Toss lightly to mix.
2. Pour into unbaked pie shell. Cover with crumbs or pastry. Bake at 400° for 10 minutes; then at 350° for 30 minutes.

Sour Cream Raspberry Pie

2 Tbsp. flour   Makes 1 9" pie
1 qt. raspberries
1 cup sour cream
2-3 Tbsp. sugar
1 9" unbaked pie shell

1. Sprinkle flour on bottom of unbaked pie shell. Fill with the raspberries. Spread sour cream over top of berries. Sprinkle with sugar.
2. Bake at 375° for 30-40 minutes until golden and bubbly.

Pies

Rhubarb Pie

3 cups diced rhubarb   Makes 1 9" pie
1¼ cups sugar
¼ tsp. salt
2 Tbsp. water
3 Tbsp. flour
1 Tbsp. lemon juice
2 eggs
1 9" unbaked pie shell

1. Place rhubarb in unbaked pie shell.
2. Combine remaining ingredients and stir to form a smooth paste.
3. Cover with crumbs made by mixing 3 Tbsp. flour, 3 Tbsp. sugar, and 2 Tbsp. butter.
4. Bake at 425° for 10 minutes; then at 325° for 30 more minutes.

Variation:
    Separate eggs and add only yolks to paste mixture. Beat whites with 2 Tbsp. sugar and ¼ tsp. cream of tartar until stiff peaks form. Instead of crumb topping, pile meringue on pie during last few minutes of baking time. Bake meringue until lightly browned.

Rhubarb-Strawberry Pie

1 pt. fresh strawberries   Makes 1 9" pie
2 cups sliced raw rhubarb
¾ cup brown sugar
½ cup sugar
1 tsp. grated lemon rind
1 double crust 9" unbaked pie shell

1. Slice strawberries and rhubarb.
2. Combine sugars and lemon rind and toss lightly with fruit. Pour into pie shell. Cover with top crust. Seal edges.
3. Bake at 350° for 50 minutes.

"Tangy and delicious!"

Pies

Fresh Strawberry
Pie or Tarts

1 qt. strawberries,   Makes 2 8" pies
   washed and hulled
¾ cup sugar (more or less if desired)
1 3oz. pkg. strawberry gelatin
1 cup hot water
1 cup whipped cream
2 8" baked pie shells, or 9 3½" baked
   tartshells

1. Combine strawberries and sugar. Let stand 10 minutes.
2. Dissolve gelatin in water. Pour all but 4 Tbsp. gelatin over berries. Chill until gelatin begins to thicken.
3. Fold 4 Tbsp. gelatin into whipped cream and chill 5-10 minutes.
4. Place a layer of whipped cream into bottom of each pie shell or tartshell and chill 10 minutes. Cover with a layer of jelled strawberries, pressing hull end of each berry lightly into cream. Add remaining thickened gelatin to fill the shells. Chill several hours before serving.

Green Tomato Pie

4 cups tomatoes   Makes 1 10" pie
2 cups brown sugar
1 tsp. cinnamon
½ tsp. cloves
1 double crust 10" unbaked pie shell

1. Wash tomatoes but do not pare. Slice in thin rings ½ hour before using. After draining for ½ hour, pour away juice.
2. Combine tomatoes, sugar, and spices.
3. Sprinkle bottom of pie crust with flour. Pour in tomato mixture. Sprinkle with flour. Cover with top crust. Seal edges.
4. Bake at 425° for 15 minutes; then at 375° for 30 minutes.

"It's spicy and delicious! My family keeps asking for it."

Mom's Mincemeat Pie

2 cups cooked beef, ground   Makes 1 9" pie
3 cups raw apples, ground
½ cup brown sugar
¼ tsp. salt
1 tsp. cinnamon
½ tsp. cloves (optional)
2 Tbsp. whiskey
4 Tbsp. Black Cherry wine
raisins (optional)
1 double crust 9" unbaked pie shell

1. Combine beef, apples, sugar, salt, and spices in saucepan. Cook over low heat till thoroughly heated. (Add beef broth if needed to keep from getting dry.)
2. Stir in whiskey, wine, and raisins.
3. Pour into unbaked pie shell. Cover with top crust. Seal edges.
4. Bake at 350° for 45 minutes. Serve hot.

"Mom's mincemeat pie is the best mincemeat pie I've ever tasted."

Variation:
Mincemeat may be frozen after step #1. To use, thaw and stir in whiskey, wine, and raisins.

Pies

Shoo Fly Pie

Crumbs:

Makes 1 9" pie

- 1 cup flour
- 1 Tbsp. shortening
- ⅔ cup light brown sugar

Cut together with 2 knives till crumbly. Take out ½ cup crumbs and set aside.

Bottom Part:

- 1 egg slightly beaten
- 1 cup molasses
- 1 cup boiling water
- 1 tsp. baking soda
- 1 9" unbaked pie shell

1. To crumb mixture add egg and molasses. Add ¾ cup boiling water. Dissolve soda in remaining ¼ cup water and add last.
2. Pour into unbaked pie shell. Sprinkle reserved crumbs on top. Bake at 425° for 15 minutes. Reduce heat to 350° and bake 40-45 minutes longer.

from
Amish and Mennonite
kitchens

Oatmeal Pie

4 eggs, slightly beaten   Makes 2 8" pies
1 cup sugar
1½ cups molasses
1 cup milk
1½ cups oatmeal
1 Tbsp. melted butter
¼ tsp. salt
2 tsp. vanilla
½ cup chopped nuts
2 8" unbaked pie shells

1. Combine all ingredients. Pour into 2 unbaked pie shells.
2. Bake at 350° for 40-45 minutes.

Montgomery Pie

Syrup: Makes 4 8" pies
juice and grated rind of 1 lemon
1 cup molasses
1 pt. water
1 cup sugar
1 Tbsp. flour
1 egg

Combine all ingredients and mix well. Divide syrup among 4 unbaked pie shells.

Pies

Top Part:
- ½ cup shortening
- 2 cups sugar
- 2 eggs
- 1 cup milk
- 2½ cups flour
- 2½ tsp. baking powder

1. Cream shortening and sugar. Add eggs and beat well.
2. Add milk alternately with flour and baking powder.
3. Divide batter and pour over the syrup in the 4 unbaked pie shells. Bake at 450° for 15 minutes; then at 350° for 45 minutes.

"This is an old family recipe from Grandma Neff's collection."

Vanilla Pie

Bottom Part:
Makes 2 9" pies

1 cup sugar
1 cup molasses
2 cups water
1 egg, well beaten
3 Tbsp. flour
1 tsp. vanilla
2 9" unbaked pie shells

1. In saucepan, combine all ingredients except vanilla. Boil until thick. Set aside to cool. When cooled, stir in vanilla. Pour into unbaked pie shells.

Crumbs:

2 cups flour
¾ cup sugar
½ cup butter or margarine
1 tsp. cream of tartar
1 tsp. soda

1. Mix all ingredients together to form crumbs. Sprinkle over tops of pies.
2. Bake at 375° for 50-60 minutes.

Grandmother Shenk's Lemon Pie

Makes 2 8" pies

1 cup sugar
¼ cup butter
2 eggs
½ cup flour
1 tsp. soda
2 cups water
Juice and grated rind of 1 lemon
2 8" unbaked pie shells

1. Cream sugar and butter. Add eggs and beat well. Add flour and soda and beat. Add water, lemon juice and grated rind and mix.
2. Pour into 2 unbaked pie shells. Bake at 425° for 15 minutes then reduce temperature to 350° and continue baking for 25-30 minutes.

"A quick and easy recipe that tastes good."

Pies

223

from
Amish and Mennonite
kitchens

Lemon Sponge Pie

Makes 1 9" pie

1 cup sugar
2 Tbsp. butter
3 eggs, separated
3 Tbsp. flour
½ tsp. salt
Juice and grated rind of 1 lemon
1½ cups hot water or milk
1 9" unbaked pie shell

1. Cream sugar and butter. Add egg yolks and beat well. Add flour, salt, lemon juice and rind. Add water or milk. Fold in stiffly beaten egg whites.
2. Pour into unbaked pie shell. Bake at 325° for 45-50 minutes.

Lemon Crumb Pie

Bottom Part:

Makes 2 9" pies

½ cup shortening
1 cup sugar
1 tsp. baking soda
3½ cups flour
¾ cup sour milk

1. Cream shortening and sugar. Add baking soda. Add flour alternately with sour milk. Batter will be stiff and sticky.

2. Roll dough ¼" thick and press into pie pans. Reserve enough dough for thin strips on top of filling.

Filling:

    1 cup sugar
    juice and grated rind of 1 lemon
    ½ cup molasses
    2 Tbsp. cornstarch
    1 cup water

1. Combine sugar, lemon, and molasses in a saucepan. Bring to a boil.

2. Combine cornstarch and water and stir till smooth. Gradually add to boiling mixture, stirring constantly. Cook till clear and slightly thickened.

3. Pour into dough-lined pie pans. Cover with strips of dough.

4. Bake at 350° for 25-30 minutes.

Pies

from
Amish and Mennonite kitchens

Old-Fashioned Baked Custard Pie

⅓ cup sugar   Makes 1 9" pie
2 tsp. flour
½ tsp. salt
3 eggs
3 cups milk
¼ tsp. nutmeg
1 9" unbaked pie shell

1. Combine sugar, flour, and salt with eggs and mix until smooth.
2. Heat milk to boiling point. And 1 cup hot milk to egg mixture and then pour into remaining hot milk.
3. Pour into unbaked pie shell. Sprinkle nutmeg over top. Bake at 350° for 40-45 minutes.

Coconut Custard Pie

2⅔ cups milk   Makes 1 9" pie
½ cup sugar
½ tsp. salt
1 tsp. vanilla
4 eggs
½ cup grated coconut
1 9" unbaked pie shell

1. Combine milk, sugar, salt, and vanilla in saucepan. Heat to scalding.
2. Beat eggs lightly. Slowly add scalded ingredients to beaten eggs.
3. Pour into unbaked pie shell. Sprinkle coconut over top of filling. Bake at 450° for 10 minutes and then at 350° for 15-20 minutes or until set.

Pies

Coconut Pie

½ cup brown sugar   Makes 1 9" pie
¼ cup flour
½ cup coconut
¼ tsp. soda
½ cup molasses
¼ cup sour cream
¾ cup milk
1 egg, beaten
1 9" unbaked pie shell

1. Combine sugar, flour, coconut, and soda. Add molasses, sour cream, milk, and beaten egg. Mix well.
2. Pour into unbaked pie shell. Bake at 350° for 10 minutes and then at 325° for 35-40 minutes.

from
Amish and Mennonite
kitchens

Peanut Butter Pie

Crumbs:
Makes 1 9" pie

⅔ cup 10x sugar
⅓ cup crunchy peanut butter

1. Mix together until fine crumbs are formed. Sprinkle ½ of crumb mixture in bottom of baked pie shell. Reserve other half of crumbs for topping.

Filling:

2 egg yolks, beaten
⅓ cup sugar
1 Tbsp. flour
1 Tbsp. cornstarch
2 cups milk
1 Tbsp. butter
1 tsp. vanilla
1 9" baked pie shell

1. Combine sugar, flour, and cornstarch. Add to beaten egg yolks. Mix to form a smooth paste. Add milk and cook, stirring constantly until thickened. Remove from heat and stir in butter and vanilla.

2. Pour partly cooled filling into baked pie shell. When cooled sprinkle with remaining crumb mixture. Serve with whipped cream.

Pecan Pie

2 Tbsp. butter   Makes 1 8" pie
¼ cup sugar
2 eggs
¾ cup molasses
1 Tbsp. flour
1 tsp. vanilla
pinch salt
¾ cup water
½ cup pecans
1 8" unbaked pie shell

1. Cream butter, sugar, and eggs. Add molasses, flour, vanilla, and salt.
2. Stir in water and pecans.
3. Pour into unbaked pie shell.
4. Bake at 450° for 10 minutes; then at 350° for 25-30 minutes.

from
Amish and Mennonite
kitchens

Walnut Custard Pie

Makes 2 8" pies

3 Tbsp. flour
½ cup water
1 cup sugar
2 eggs, beaten
¾ cup King Syrup molasses
1½ cups milk
1½ cups walnuts
2 8" baked pie shells

1. Combine flour and water and stir to make a smooth paste. Add sugar, eggs, molasses, and milk.
2. Cook over medium high heat until thickened, stirring constantly.
3. Cool. Add walnuts. Pour into baked pie shells. Allow to stand for several hours before cutting.

"Rich ... and chewy."

Cheese Pie

1 - 8 oz. pkg. cream cheese   Makes 1 10" pie
2 eggs, separated
¾ cup sugar
2 Tbsp. flour
dash of salt
½ tsp. vanilla
1 cup evaporated milk
1 cup sweet milk
1 10" unbaked pie shell

1. Soften cream cheese. In mixing bowl combine cheese, egg yolks, sugar, flour, salt, and vanilla. Beat until smooth.
2. Add evaporated milk a bit at a time and beat till smooth. Gradually add remaining milk.
3. Fold in stiffly beaten egg whites.
4. Pour into chilled, unbaked pie shell. Bake for 15 minutes at 400°; then 15 minutes at 375°; then 15 minutes at 325°.

"This is delicious served with molasses."

Pies

Thick Milk Pie

Makes 2 9" pies

3 eggs
1 cup molasses
1 cup sugar
½ cup flour
1 tsp. soda
3 cups thick, sour milk
2 9" unbaked pie shells

1. Beat eggs. Add molasses.
2. Combine sugar, flour, and soda and add to egg mixture. Add thick milk. Pour into 2 unbaked pie shells.
3. Bake at 400° for 10 minutes; then at 325° for 40-45 minutes.

Variation:
Sprinkle top of pie with cinnamon.

"Yummy... delicious! Tastes like pumpkin, coconut, and shoo fly pie!"

Raisin Pie

Pies

2 cups raisins   *Makes 1 9" pie*
2 cups cold water
1½ cups sugar
4 Tbsp. flour
2 eggs, separated
¼ tsp. salt
4 Tbsp. melted butter
1 Tbsp. vinegar or lemon juice
1 9" baked pie shell

1. In saucepan combine raisins, 1½ cups water and 1 cup sugar and bring to a boil. Combine the remaining ½ cup water and ½ cup sugar, plus flour, egg yolks, and salt; add to raisin mixture. Cook until thickened, stirring constantly. Remove from heat and add butter and vinegar or lemon juice.
2. Pour mixture into baked pie shell. Cover with whipped cream or meringue.

Meringue:

Beat egg whites till stiff peaks form. Gradually add 2 Tbsp. sugar while beating. Pile on top of pie and bake at 350° till golden brown, about 10 minutes.

Ground-Cherry Pie

2½ cups ground-cherries   Makes 1 8" pie
½ cup brown sugar
1 Tbsp. flour
1 Tbsp. minute tapioca
3 Tbsp. water
2 Tbsp. butter or margarine
1 two-crust unbaked 8" pie shell

1. Wash ground-cherries and place in unbaked pie shell. Mix sugar, flour, and tapioca and sprinkle over cherries. Dribble water over top. Dot with butter or margarine.
2. Cover with top crust. Seal edges.
3. Bake 15 minutes at 400°; reduce temperature to 375° and bake 30 minutes longer.

Ground-cherries are a fruit distinct from the more common sweet cherries and sour cherries. They grow on low bushes; each cherry is encased in a paper-like pod.

Never Fail Pie Crust

3 cups flour   Makes 4 9" pie shells
1 tsp. salt
1¼ cup vegetable shortening
1 egg, beaten
⅓ cup cold water
1 Tbsp. vinegar

1. Mix flour and salt. Cut in shortening.
2. Combine remaining ingredients and stir into shortening mixture. Let stand a few minutes.
3. Roll dough on floured board to desired thickness.

Snails

1. Use left over pie dough. Roll out, spread with butter, brown sugar, and cinnamon.
2. Roll up like a jelly roll, slice and bake at 375° for 12 minutes or until brown.

Cakes

from
Amish and Mennonite
kitchens

Cakes

Eat a banana or eggs with warm shoo-fly cake and you have a breakfast. Dollop the cake with whipped cream and you have dessert.

In the Pennsylvania Dutch world, cakes turn up at breakfast, in lunch boxes and at company dinners. Cakes are treats, but then they're also part of daily fare. The special part.

Most cooks have a cake or two they're famous for—moist chocolate with caramel icing, oatmeal, spice. But a covered dish lunch at church or a family reunion become occasions to try out a new recipe— pumpkin chiffon, perhaps, or black walnut.

A word about the number of angel food and chiffon cakes in our collection— traditionally most families had chickens on their homesteads, so eggs were plentiful. Cakes, rich in eggs, were not a luxury. But when the chickens were sold, neither the preference for light, airy cakes nor the joy of their memory disappeared!

If these favorites don't conjure up a memory for you, they'll create one!

Shoo-Fly Cake

4 cups flour (use 2   Makes 1 long cake
   cups whole wheat flour and 2 cups
   white flour if desired)
2 cups brown sugar
1 cup butter or margarine
2 cups boiling water
1 cup molasses
2 tsp. baking soda

1. Work the flour, sugar, and butter into
fine crumbs with your fingers or a pastry
mixer. Set aside 1½ cups crumbs for topping.
2. Mix water, molasses, and baking soda
together. Then add to the remaining crumbs.
Mix until batter is very thin yet still lumpy.
3. Pour into greased and floured 9"x13"
cake pan. Sprinkle with reserved crumbs.
Bake at 350° for 35 minutes.

"Best served slightly warm, fresh from
the oven."

Cakes

Moist Chocolate Cake

2 cups flour, sifted
2 cups sugar
¾ cup cocoa
2 tsp. baking soda
1 tsp. baking powder
pinch salt
½ cup oil
1 cup hot coffee
1 cup milk
2 eggs

1. Mix together flour, sugar, cocoa, baking soda and powder, and salt.
2. Make a well in the center of the dry ingredients and add oil, coffee, milk, and eggs. Beat just enough to mix well. (Batter will be lumpy.)
3. Pour into a greased 9"x 13" cake pan and bake 35 minutes at 350°.
4. Spread slightly warm cake with Quick Carmel Frosting (or any other favorite!).

Mother Pellman's Chocolate Cake

1½ cups sugar
½ cup vegetable oil
   or margarine
2 eggs
½ cup sour milk or buttermilk
3 heaping Tbsp. cocoa (scant ½ cup)
1 cup boiling water
2½ cups all-purpose flour, sifted
2 tsp. baking powder
1 tsp. baking soda
¼ tsp. salt
1 tsp. vanilla

Makes 1 layer or 1 long cake

1. Cream the sugar and shortening together until lemon-colored. Then beat in eggs and sour milk or buttermilk.
2. Pour boiling water over cocoa and stir until it thickens slightly. Add to the creamed mixture.
3. Add flour, baking powder, soda, salt, and vanilla and beat well.
4. Pour into a greased and floured 9"x 13" pan or two 9" layer pans. Bake 20~25 minutes at 350°.

Chocolate Cake Roll

Makes 10-12 servings

3 eggs, separated
1 cup sugar
⅓ cup water
1 cup flour
1 tsp. baking powder
confectioner's sugar
2 Tbsp. cocoa
2 Tbsp. cornstarch
¾ cup sugar
1 cup cold water
1 Tbsp. butter or margarine
½ tsp. vanilla

1. Beat 3 egg yolks, 1 cup sugar, and water together until light. Slowly beat in flour and baking powder.
2. Beat 3 egg whites until stiff peaks form. Fold flour and egg mixture carefully into beaten whites.
3. Pour into greased and floured jelly roll pan. Bake at 425° for 8 minutes.
4. Loosen hot cake from sides of pan and invert on a cotton towel dusted with confectioner's sugar. While cake is still hot, roll up in the towel for a few minutes, then unroll.
5. Stir cocoa, cornstarch, sugar, and water

together in a saucepan. Heat until mixture comes to a boil.

6. Remove from heat. Stir in butter and vanilla. Cool. Then spread on cake. Roll cake, slice (¼" slices) and serve. Sprinkle with confectioner's sugar, if desired, before serving.

Cakes

Quick Carmel Frosting

½ cup butter or margarine
1 cup brown sugar
¼ cup milk
1¾-2 cups sifted confectioner's sugar

1. Melt butter in saucepan. Add brown sugar and cook over low heat two minutes, stirring constantly.
2. Add milk and continue stirring until mixture comes to a boil.
3. Remove from heat and cool. Add confectioner's sugar until frosting reaches spreading consistency.

from
Amish and Mennonite
kitchens

"Lovelight" Chocolate Chiffon Cake

2 eggs, separated   Makes 1 layer or
1½ cups sugar   long cake
1¾ cups cake flour, sifted
¾ tsp. baking soda
¾ tsp. salt
4 Tbsp. cocoa
⅓ cup vegetable oil
1 cup buttermilk

1. Beat egg whites until frothy. Gradually add ½ cup sugar. Beat mixture until very stiff. Set aside.
2. Sift remaining sugar, flour, soda, salt, and cocoa into another bowl. Add oil and half of buttermilk. Beat 1 minute with mixer.
3. Add remaining buttermilk and egg yolks and beat one more minute. Fold in egg white mixture.
4. Pour into 2 greased and floured 8" round cake pans or 1 9"x 13" baking pan. Bake at 350° for 35~40 minutes.

244

Chocolate Angel Food Cake

Makes 1 tube cake

1¼ cups egg whites
¼ tsp. salt
1 tsp. cream of tartar
1¼ cups granulated sugar, sifted
¾ cup cake flour, sifted
4 Tbsp. cocoa
1 tsp. vanilla

1. Beat egg whites, salt, and cream of tartar until the whites mixture stands in peaks.
2. Gradually fold in sugar.
3. Fold in very gradually, a tablespoon or two at a time, the sifted flour and cocoa mixture. Then gently add the vanilla.
4. When well blended, pour into an ungreased tube pan and bake at 275° for 30 minutes, then increase temperature to 325° and bake for 30~45 minutes longer.

Cakes

245

Hot Milk Sponge Cake

Makes 1 long cake

2 cups cake flour
2 tsp. baking powder
½ tsp. salt
4 eggs
2 tsp. vanilla
2 cups granulated sugar
1 cup milk
2 Tbsp. butter

1. Sift flour, baking powder, and salt together.
2. Beat eggs and vanilla together; then gradually add sugar and continue beating until mixture becomes light and lemon colored.
3. Blend dry ingredients into creamed mixture.
4. Bring milk and butter to the boiling point; then quickly stir into batter. Blend well.
5. Pour quickly into a 13"x 9"x 2" baking pan which has been greased and floured on the bottom only. Bake at 350° for 35-40 minutes.

Variations:
    1. Add ½ tsp. almond extract to the egg and vanilla mixture.
    2. Add 1 tsp. lemon flavoring and 1 tsp. orange flavoring to the egg and vanilla mixture.

Cakes

Short Cake

  2 cups flour   Makes 4-6 servings
  2 Tbsp. sugar
  ½ tsp. salt
  2½ tsp. baking powder
  4 Tbsp. margarine
  1 cup milk

1. Stir dry ingredients together; then cut in margarine.
2. Add milk and mix well until batter is quite stiff.
3. Spread batter in round cake pan or on a cookie sheet, about ¾" thick.
4. Bake at 325° until golden in color, but not brown.

from
Amish and Mennonite
kitchens

Chiffon Cake

2 cups cake flour,   Makes 1 tube pan cake
   sifted
1½ cups sugar
3 tsp. baking powder
1 tsp. salt
½ cup vegetable oil
7 egg yolks, unbeaten
¾ cup cold water
2 tsp. vanilla
2 tsp. lemon rind, grated
½ tsp. cream of tartar
7 egg whites

1. Sift flour, sugar, baking powder, and salt together two or three times.
2. Mix oil, egg yolks, water, vanilla, and lemon rind together well; then add to the dry ingredients and blend until smooth.
3. Add cream of tartar to egg whites; then beat until very stiff, but not dry.
4. Pour the creamed mixture in a thin stream over the egg whites; then fold gently together until well blended.
5. Pour into an ungreased tube pan. Bake at 325° for 65 minutes. Turn off oven, but do not remove cake for another 5

minutes.

6. Remove cake from oven and invert pan until cake cools.

Variation:
Add 1 tsp. cinnamon, ½ tsp. ground cloves, ½ tsp. nutmeg and a dash of allspice to the dry ingredients before sifting.

Crumb Cake

3 cups flour   Makes 1 long cake
2 cups brown sugar
½ cup shortening, butter or margarine
1 egg, beaten
1 cup buttermilk
1 tsp. baking soda
1 tsp. cream of tarter

1. Mix flour and brown sugar together. Cut in shortening until mixture is crumbly. Take out 1 cup crumbs for topping.
2. Add to remaining crumbs, the next 4 ingredients in the order they are listed. Mix well after each addition.
3. Pour into a greased 9"x13" baking pan. Sprinkle reserved cup of crumbs over top. Bake at 375° for 25-30 minutes.

Pumpkin Chiffon Cake

2 cups cake flour,   Makes 1 tube pan cake
    sifted
1½ cups sugar
3 tsp. baking powder
1 tsp. cinnamon
½ tsp. ground nutmeg
½ tsp. ground cloves
½ cup vegetable oil
8 egg yolks
½ cup water
¾ cup canned or cooked mashed pumpkin
½ tsp. cream of tartar
8 egg whites

1. Sift all dry ingredients into a large mixing bowl.
2. Make a deep well in the center. Add, in order, salad oil, egg yolks, water, and pumpkin. Beat until satiny smooth.
3. Add the cream of tartar to the egg whites. Beat until very stiff, but not dry.
4. Pour the pumpkin mixture in a thin stream over the egg whites; then gently fold into the whites with a spatula.
5. Bake in an ungreased tube pan 55 minutes at 325°. Then increase heat to

350° and bake 10 more minutes.

6. Invert pan until cake cools. Remove from pan and cover with maple frosting and nuts.

Cream Cheese Frosting

    4 Tbsp. butter or margarine, softened
    3 oz. package Philadelphia cream cheese, softened
    2 cups confectioner's sugar
    1 tsp. vanilla

1. Beat together until smooth.
2. Spread on slightly warm cake.

Quick Sugar and Cinnamon Coffee Cake

1½ cups cake flour, sifted   Makes 1 square cake

¼ tsp. salt

2 tsp. baking powder

⅔ cup sugar

¼ cup shortening, melted

1 egg

½ cup milk

½ tsp. vanilla

1. Sift dry ingredients together. Add remaining ingredients.

2. Beat altogether in electric mixer on number 3 speed, about 2 minutes. Scrape sides and bottom of bowl while beating.

3. Pour batter into 8" square baking pan or a deep 9" layer cake pan. Bake at 350° for 25 minutes. Remove from oven and put on Topping.

Topping

4 Tbsp. butter or margarine, melted

¼ cup sugar

½ tsp. cinnamon

1. Brush warm cake with butter.
2. Mix sugar and cinnamon together. Sprinkle over top.
3. Return cake to oven and bake 5 minutes longer.

Black Walnut Cake

¾ cup shortening
1¼ cups brown sugar
3 eggs
1½ cups buttermilk
2¾ cups flour
1⅓ tsp. baking soda
½ tsp. allspice
1 tsp. salt
1 cup black walnuts, chopped

Makes 1 layer or 1 long cake

1. Cream shortening and sugar together. Add eggs and beat until lemon-colored.
2. Sift together dry ingredients. Add them alternately with the buttermilk to the creamed mixture, beating well after each addition.
3. Stir in the walnuts.
4. Pour batter into greased 9" x 13" pan or two 9" round layer pans. Bake 35~40 minutes at 350°.

German Apple Cake

Makes 1 long cake

½ cup shortening
1 cup sugar
½ cup brown sugar
2 eggs
2¼ cups flour
2 tsp. cinnamon
2 tsp. baking soda
1 cup sour milk
2 cups raw apples, peeled and diced

1. Beat shortening until smooth. Add sugars and eggs and beat until fluffy.
2. Mix flour and cinnamon together. Combine soda and sour milk. Then add the dry ingredients and the milk alternately to the creamed mixture.
3. When well blended, fold in apples.
4. Pour into greased 9"x 13" cake pan. Sprinkle topping over cake and then bake at 350° for 45-50 minutes.

Topping

½ cup brown sugar
¼ cup sugar
½ tsp. cinnamon
½ cup chopped nuts or coconut

Hannah's Raisin Cake

2 cups boiling water
1 lb. raisins
½ cup shortening
2 cups sugar
1 cup buttermilk or sour milk
½ tsp. salt
1 tsp. cinnamon
½ tsp. cloves
1 Tbsp. baking soda
4 cups flour

Makes 1 layer or tube cake

1. Pour boiling water over raisins in sauce pan. Boil 15 minutes. Let cool.
2. Cream shortening and sugar together. Add buttermilk.
3. Combine all dry ingredients; then add to creamy mixture. When well blended, stir in raisins.
4. Bake at 350° for 30~45 minutes in either 2 layer pans or a tube pan.

Raw Apple Cake

Makes 1 long cake

1 cup sugar
1 cup vegetable oil
3 eggs
1 tsp. vanilla
1½ cups flour
½ cup whole wheat flour
1 tsp. cinnamon
1 tsp. soda
1 tsp. salt
5 cups raw apples, diced
½ cup nuts, chopped
½ tsp. cinnamon
¼ cup sugar

1. Blend first 4 ingredients together in mixing bowl. Add the next 5 ingredients and stir well.
2. Fold in the apples and nuts.
3. Spread batter in greased 9" x 13" baking pan.
4. Mix together cinnamon and sugar and sprinkle over batter.
5. Bake at 350° for 45 minutes.

Blueberry Cake

¾ cup sugar
¼ cup vegetable oil
1 egg
½ cup milk
2 cups flour
2 tsp. baking powder
½ tsp. salt
2 cups blueberries, well drained

Makes 9~12 servings

1. Cream together the sugar, oil, and egg until lemon~colored. Stir in milk, thoroughly.
2. Sift together the flour, baking powder, and salt and stir into creamed mixture.
3. Gently fold in the blueberries.
4. Spread batter into a greased and floured 9"x 9" square baking pan. Sprinkle with topping. Bake 45~50 minutes at 375°. Serve warm.

Topping

¼ cup butter or margarine
½ cup granulated sugar
⅓ cup flour
½ tsp. cinnamon

1. Melt butter. Stir in sugar, flour, and cinnamon.
2. Crumble over cake batter.

Cakes

Carrot Cake

Makes 1 long cake

3 eggs
2 cups flour, sifted
2 cups sugar
1¼ cups vegetable oil
2 tsp. baking soda
1 tsp. cinnamon
1 tsp. salt
2 tsp. vanilla
1 cup shredded coconut
1 cup walnuts, chopped
1 cup crushed pineapple, drained
2 cups raw carrot, shredded

1. Beat eggs well; then add the next seven ingredients and beat well until smooth.
2. Stir in the coconut, nuts, pineapple, and carrots with a mixing spoon.
3. Pour into a greased 9"x 13" cake pan and bake at 350° for 50 minutes.
4. When cake is slightly warm, spread with Cream Cheese Frosting, (page 251).

Pumpkin Cake

4 eggs, well beaten
2 cups sugar
1½ cups vegetable oil
3 cups flour
3 tsp. baking powder
2 tsp. cinnamon
2 tsp. baking soda
¼ tsp. salt
½ tsp. ginger
2 cups pumpkin
1 cup walnuts, chopped

Makes 1 layer or
long cake

Cakes

1. To the beaten eggs add the sugar and blend well. Beat in oil.
2. Add the dry ingredients and pumpkin and mix thoroughly. Stir in walnuts by hand.
3. Pour batter into well greased and floured 9"x 13" baking pan or 2 round 9" pans. Bake at 350° for 45-60 minutes (test center with pick to be sure cake is fully baked).
4. Frost with Cream Cheese Icing on page 251.

Zucchini Squash Cake

Makes 1 tube cake

4 eggs
2 cups sugar
1 cup vegetable oil
2 cups flour
2 tsp. cinnamon
2 tsp. baking powder
1 tsp. baking soda
1 tsp. salt
1 can (8¼ oz.) crushed pineapple,
    well drained
1 cup walnuts, chopped
2 cups grated raw (or frozen) unpeeled
    zucchini squash
2 tsp. vanilla

1. In a large mixing bowl beat the eggs and sugar together until lemon-colored. Add vegetable oil and beat until well blended.
2. In a separate bowl sift together the flour, cinnamon, baking powder, baking soda, and salt. Add dry ingredients to creamed mixture and beat two minutes.
3. Stir in pineapple, walnuts, zucchini (squeeze in a paper towel to remove excess moisture), and vanilla. Mix thoroughly.

4. Pour batter into a well greased and floured 10" tube pan. Bake at 350° for 1 hour and 20 minutes. Cool on rack for 30 minutes and remove from pan.
5. Glaze cake, if desired, with 1 cup confectioner's sugar mixed with 1 Tbsp. milk.

Banana Cake

4 cups ripe banana,   Makes 1 long cake
    cut fine
2 eggs, beaten
1½ cups sugar
½ cup oil
1 tsp. vanilla
½ cup nuts, chopped
2 cups flour
2 tsp. baking soda
1 tsp. salt

1. Cream banana, eggs, sugar, oil, and vanilla together until smooth. Stir in nuts.
2. Sift together flour, baking soda, and salt.
3. Add dry ingredients to creamed mixture, blending just until all ingredients are moistened. Do not over mix.
4. Bake at 350° for 40~45 minutes in a 9"x 13" pan.

Hot Applesauce Cake

½ cup shortening   Makes 1 loaf cake
1⅓ cups sugar
2 eggs
2 cups flour
1 tsp. cinnamon
½ tsp. nutmeg
¼ tsp. ground cloves
1 cup hot applesauce
1 tsp. baking soda dissolved in
      2 Tbsp. hot water
1 cup raisins
⅓ cup walnuts, chopped

1. Cream shortening and sugar together until fluffy. Blend eggs in thoroughly.
2. Sift dry ingredients together. Add them alternately with the hot applesauce to the creamed mixture. Beat well after each addition.
3. Add soda dissolved in water and mix well.
4. Flour raisins and nuts lightly and fold into mixture.
5. Bake in a greased 5"x 9"x 4" loaf pan at 350° for 1 hour and 10 minutes, or until firm in the middle when tested with a toothpick.

Mandarin Orange Cake

2 eggs   Makes 1 long cake
2 11 oz. cans mandarin oranges,
   well drained
2 cups flour
2 cups sugar
2 tsp. baking soda
½ tsp. salt

1. Beat eggs. Add oranges and dry ingredients. Beat 4 minutes with electric mixer
on slow speed until oranges flake through the
batter. Pour into greased 9"x13" cake pan.
2. Bake at 350° for 35-40 minutes. Cake
will get quite dark. Before removing from
oven, press top with finger tip to see if it
bounces back. If it doesn't, bake a bit longer,
taking care that it doesn't burn.
3. Remove cake from oven. Pour topping
over. Return cake to oven and bake 5
minutes longer.

Topping

¾ cup brown sugar
3 Tbsp. milk
2 Tbsp. butter or margarine

Combine and bring to a rolling boil.

Cakes

Oatmeal Cake

Makes 1 long cake

1¼ cups boiling water
1 cup oatmeal
½ cup margarine, softened
1 cup brown sugar
1 cup granulated sugar
2 eggs
1½ cups flour
1 tsp. baking soda
2 tsp. baking powder
1 tsp. cinnamon
1 tsp. salt

1. Pour boiling water over oatmeal. Set aside.
2. Cream together margarine, sugars, and eggs. Then add oatmeal mixture and the remaining ingredients.
3. Pour batter into a greased 9"x13" baking pan and bake at 350° for 30 minutes.
4. Cool cake and spread with Topping (page 265). Put under broiler until topping bubbles, about 2 minutes.

Out-of-This-World Cake

2 cups sugar   Makes 1 loaf cake
½ lb. butter or margarine, softened
4 eggs
1 cup milk
2 tsp. baking powder
3⅓ cups graham cracker crumbs
1 cup coconut
1 cup nuts
1 20 oz. can crushed pineapple   drained

1. Beat first 6 ingredients together well. Then fold in the coconut, nuts, and pineapple.
2. Pour into a greased 9"x13" baking pan and bake at 350° for 1 hour.

Topping

¼ cup butter or margarine, softened
⅔ cup brown sugar
¼ cup milk
1 cup coconut
1 cup pecans, chopped

Mix together and spread on cake. Return cake to oven and bake 5 minutes or until topping bubbles and is slightly browned.

Cakes

Spice Cake

2 cups brown sugar
½ cup butter
2 eggs
1 cup sour milk
2½ cups sifted flour
1½ tsp. baking powder
1 tsp. cinnamon
1 tsp. nutmeg
1 tsp. baking soda
1 tsp. vanilla

Makes 1 layer cake
or 1 long cake

1. Cream sugar and butter together until fluffy.
2. Add eggs and beat until light.
3. Sift together all dry ingredients; then add them alternately with the milk to the creamed mixture, beating well after each addition. Then mix in the vanilla.
4. Pour into greased layer pans or a 9" x 13" cake pan. Bake at 350° for 35-40 minutes.

Party Angel Food Cake

1 cup and 2 Tbsp. Makes 1 tube cake
    cake flour, sifted
¾ cup sugar
1⅔ cups egg whites (about 12)
1½ tsp. cream of tartar
½ tsp. salt
1 tsp. vanilla
½ tsp. almond flavoring
¾ cup sugar
½ cup pecans, chopped

1. Sift the flour and ¾ cup sugar together four times. Set aside.
2. Combine egg whites, cream of tartar, salt, vanilla, and almond flavoring and beat until the whites are stiff but not dry.
3. Add ¾ cup sugar, 2 tablespoons at a time, folding it in well each time.
4. Then add flour~sugar mixture in four parts, folding in the additions with 15 strokes each time.
5. Finally, fold in the pecans.
6. Pour into an ungreased 10" tube pan; then gently draw a thin spatula through the batter to break any large air bubbles. Bake at 350° for 45 minutes. Invert and cool.

Cakes

Cookies

from
Amish and Mennonite
kitchens

from
Amish and Mennonite
kitchens

Cookies

What simpler pleasure than a warm, freshly baked cookie?

And with the best cookies go memories... "Mom always baked hermits for Christmas..." "Grandma let me put the raisins on the sugar cookies she baked for market..." "We'd make chocolate whoopie pies for the bake stand at the farm auction every fall..." "Nothing like peanut butter cookies and cold lemonade to break up a hot afternoon of working in the field."

Most mothers and grandmothers have their specialties. They serve them up with love and only one restriction: "No cookies before mealtime!" Otherwise they're kept in store for whenever stomachs growl.

These recipes are favorites, most of them several generations old!

Chocolate Chip Cookies

Makes about 8 dozen

1 cup shortening
2 cups sugar
4 eggs
1 cup sour cream
4 cups flour
½ tsp. salt
2 tsp. soda
1 or 2 packs chocolate chips
1 cup chopped nuts
2 cups raisins (boiled, cooled, and drained),
    optional

1. Cream shortening and sugar.
2 Add eggs and beat till fluffy. Add sour cream and mix well. Gradually add flour, salt, and soda. Mix well.
3. Stir in chocolate chips, nuts, and raisins, if desired.
4. Drop by heaping teaspoons onto greased cookie sheet. Bake at 375° for 10 minutes.

They are more moist when they are kept in the freezer a while.

"The most delicious cookies I've ever made! They taste more-ish. I didn't get a chance to put any in the freezer."

Cookies

from
Amish and Mennonite
kitchens

Amish Cookies

Makes 7½ dozen

2½ cups sugar
1⅛ cups shortening
3 eggs
⅔ cup dark molasses
1 cup sour milk
6½ cups flour
2 Tbsp. baking powder
3 Tbsp. cinnamon
2 Tbsp. soda
1½ tsp. nutmeg
2 cups oatmeal
1 cup raisins
¾ cup chopped peanuts or walnuts

1. Cream sugar and shortening. Add eggs and beat well.
2. Add milk and molasses alternately with sifted dry ingredients.
3. Add oatmeal, raisins, and nuts. Mix with hands. Bake at 350° for 8-10 minutes.

Hermits

1 cup shortening	Makes about 10 dozen

1 cup sugar
1 cup brown sugar
4 eggs
½ cup molasses
1 tsp. baking soda dissolved in
½ cup warm water
4½ cups flour
¼ tsp. salt
½ tsp. ground cloves
1 cup chopped nuts
1 cup chopped dates

1. Cream shortening and sugars.
2. Add eggs and beat until light and fluffy.
3. Sift dry ingredients and add alternately with water and molasses. Beat after each addition.
4. Stir in chopped nuts and dates.
5. Drop by rounded teaspoons onto greased cookie sheet. Bake at 350° for 10-12 minutes.

Variation:

Use ½ cup cooled black coffee instead of water. Add 1 cup raisins and 1 cup chopped dried apricots in place of nuts and dates.

Cookies

from
Amish and Mennonite
kitchens

Date Balls

1 cup sugar   Makes 3 dozen
½ cup butter
dash of salt
1 cup chopped dates
1 egg, beaten
1 cup chopped pecans
2 cups Rice Krispies cereal
coconut

1. Heat first three ingredients over low heat until butter is melted.
2. Add dates and beaten egg and bring to boil. Boil 5 minutes, stirring constantly.
3. Cool. Add pecans and cereal. Form balls 1½ inch in diameter. Roll in coconut.

Snickerdoodles

1 cup shortening   Makes 4 dozen
1½ cups sugar
2 eggs
2¾ cups flour
2 tsp. cream of tartar
1 tsp. soda
½ tsp. salt

Cookies

1. Cream shortening and sugar. Add eggs and beat well.
2. Sift together flour, cream of tartar, soda, and salt. Gradually stir into creamed mixture.
3. Chill dough 2 hours or more. Form into balls the size of walnuts. Roll each ball in a mixture of 2 Tbsp. sugar and 2 tsp. cinnamon. Bake at 400° for about 10 minutes. (Cookies should be lightly browned but still soft.)

Shrewberry Cookies

2¼ cups brown sugar   *Makes 6 dozen*
¾ cup shortening
4 eggs
4 cups flour
1 tsp. soda
1 tsp. nutmeg
1 tsp. cinnamon
1 tsp. cloves

1. Cream sugar and shortening. Add eggs and beat well.
2. Add flour, soda, and spices and mix well.
3. Drop by rounded teaspoons onto cookie sheet. Sprinkle with sugar. Bake at 375° for 10-12 minutes.

Peanut Butter Cookies

Makes 5 dozen

1 cup sugar
1 cup brown sugar
1 cup butter or 1 cup shortening
1 cup peanut butter
2 eggs
1 tsp. soda
½ tsp. salt
1 tsp. vanilla
3 cups flour

1. Cream sugars and shortening. Add peanut butter and mix well. Add eggs and mix well.
2. Add soda, salt, and vanilla. Gradually add flour.
3. Roll into balls and place 2 inches apart on cookie sheet. Flatten balls with fork dipped in flour to prevent sticking. Bake at 375° for 10-12 minutes.

"So buttery they melt in your mouth!"

Oatmeal Peanut Butter Cookies

Makes 5½ dozen

1 cup sugar
1 cup brown sugar
1 cup shortening
1 cup peanut butter
3 eggs
1½ cups flour
1 tsp. soda
1 tsp. salt
1 tsp. vanilla
2 cups quick oats
1 cup chocolate morsels or raisins

1. Cream sugars and shortening. Add eggs and peanut butter and beat well.
2. Gradually add flour, salt, and soda. Add vanilla. Stir in quick oats and chocolate morsels or raisins.
3. Drop by heaping teaspoons onto cookie sheet. Bake at 350° for 15 minutes.

"These cookies disappear fast. They're like 2 good cookies in 1."

Cookies

Filled Oatmeal Cookies

Makes 3 dozen

1 cup sugar
1 cup shortening
2 cups oatmeal (grind in blender)
2 cups flour
½ tsp. soda
½ tsp. salt
½ cup sour milk

1. Cream sugar and shortening.
2. Combine dry ingredients and add alternately with sour milk. Mix well.
3. Roll ¼-½ inch thick on floured board. Cut with round cookie cutter and bake at 350° for 10-12 minutes.

Filling

1 cup sugar
1 cup water
2 cups dates (ground or finely chopped)

1. Combine ingredients in saucepan and cook 20-30 minutes until thickened.
2. Place a spoonful of filling between 2 cookies and press firmly together.

Variation:

Sweet milk may be used in place of sour milk. Omit baking soda and add 3 tsp. baking powder.

Oatmeal Cookies

1 cup brown sugar　　　　Makes 5 dozen
½ cup sugar
¾ cup shortening
1 egg
¼ cup water
1 tsp. vanilla
1 tsp. salt
½ tsp. soda
1½ cups flour
3 cups oats (old fashioned or quick cooking)

1. Cream sugars and shortening. Add egg, water, and vanilla and beat until creamy.
2. Sift together flour, soda, and salt and add to creamed mixture. Mix well. Stir in oats.
3. Drop by heaping teaspoons onto greased cookie sheet. Bake at 350° for 10-15 minutes.

Variation:

Chopped nuts, raisins, chocolate chips, or coconut may also be added.

from
**Amish and Mennonite
kitchens**

Oatmeal Whoopie Pies

2 cups brown sugar   Makes 3 dozen
¾ cup butter or shortening   sandwich pies
2 eggs
½ tsp. salt
1 tsp. cinnamon
1 tsp. baking powder
3 Tbsp. boiling water
1 tsp. soda
2 ½ cups flour
2 cups oatmeal

1. Cream sugar and shortening.
2. Add eggs ; then add salt, cinnamon, and baking powder. Add soda dissolved in hot water. Gradually add flour and oatmeal.
3. Drop batter by heaping teaspoons onto greased cookie sheet. Bake at 350° for 8-10 minutes or until brown.

Filling

1 egg white, beaten   1 tsp. vanilla
2 Tbsp. milk   1 cup 10x sugar

1. Mix ; then add one more cup 10x sugar and ¾ cup shortening.

2. Spread dab of filling on flat side of cooled cookie. Top with another cookie to form a sandwich pie.

Chocolate Whoopie Pies

2 cups sugar
1 cup shortening
2 eggs
4 cups flour
1 cup baking cocoa
2 tsp. vanilla
1 tsp. salt
1 cup sour milk
2 tsp. baking soda
1 cup hot water

Makes 4 dozen
sandwich pies

1. Cream sugar and shortening. Add eggs.
2. Sift together flour, cocoa, and salt. Add alternately with sour milk. Add vanilla. Dissolve soda in hot water and add last. Mix well.
3. Drop by rounded teaspoons onto cookie sheet. Bake at 400° for 8-10 minutes.
4. Make sandwiches from 2 cookies filled with Whoopie Pie Filling. Recipe for filling will need to be doubled for this batch of cookies (see page 280).

from
Amish and Mennonite
kitchens

Pumpkin Whoopie Pies

2 cups brown sugar	Makes 3 dozen
1 cup vegetable oil	sandwich pies

1½ cups cooked, mashed pumpkin
2 eggs
3 cups flour
1 tsp. salt
1 tsp. baking powder
1 tsp. baking soda
1 tsp. vanilla
1½ Tbsp. cinnamon
½ Tbsp. ginger
½ Tbsp. ground cloves

1. Cream sugar and oil.
2. Add pumpkin and eggs. Add flour, salt, baking powder, soda, vanilla, and spices. Mix well.
3. Drop by heaping teaspoons onto greased cookie sheet. Bake at 350° for 10-12 minutes.
4. Make sandwiches from 2 cookies filled with the Whoopie Pie Filling recipe on page 280.

Variation:
   Adding ½ cup black walnuts (ground) gives these cookies a special delicious flavor.

Gingersnaps

Makes 11 dozen

3 cups sugar
2¼ cups shortening
3 eggs
¾ cup molasses
3 Tbsp. ground ginger
3 tsp. cinnamon
6 tsp. baking soda
1½ tsp. salt
6½ cups flour

1. Cream sugar and shortening. Add eggs and molasses and beat well. Add spices, soda, and salt. Mix well.
2. Gradually add flour. Dough will become very stiff and may need to be mixed by hand.
3. Form 1 inch balls from dough. Roll each ball in sugar and place 2 inches apart on cookie sheet. Do not flatten. Bake at 350° for 12-15 minutes.

"They should not be overly brown when you take them out of the oven, and will be puffed up a bit, but will get 'snappy' when cooled."

Cookies

from
Amish and Mennonite
kitchens

Gingerbread Men

Makes 3 dozen

1 cup margarine
1 cup sugar
½ cup dark molasses
1 tsp. cinnamon
1 tsp. nutmeg
1 tsp. cloves
1 tsp. ginger
2 eggs
1 tsp. vinegar
5 cups flour
1 tsp. baking soda
raisins and cinnamon candies

1. In saucepan cream margarine and sugar. Add molasses and spices. Mix well. Bring to boil, constantly stirring. Remove from heat and cool.
2. Stir in well-beaten eggs and vinegar. Sift flour and baking soda and stir into molasses mixture to form a smooth dough.
3. Chill several hours. Divide dough into 6 portions. Roll out on aluminum foil. Cut with gingerbread man cutter. Remove excess dough. Garnish with raisins for eyes and buttons and cinnamon candies for mouth.
4. Place foil and men on cookie sheet and bake at 350° for 8-10 minutes.

Ginger Cookies

1 cup dark brown sugar *Makes 4½ dozen*
½ cup shortening
1 egg
½ cup Brer Rabbit molasses
1 tsp. ginger
1½ tsp. cinnamon
3 cups flour
½ tsp. salt
1½ tsp. soda
1 cup sour milk
½ tsp. vanilla

1. Cream sugar and shortening. Add egg, molasses, ginger, and cinnamon.
2. Sift flour, soda, and salt. Add alternately with sour milk. Add vanilla. Chill dough several hours.
3. Drop by teaspoons onto cookie sheet. Bake at 400° for 6-8 minutes.

"I bake these at Christmas and sprinkle red and green sugar on top."

from
Amish and Mennonite
kitchens

Caramel Cookies

2 cups brown sugar   Makes 5½ dozen
½ cup butter
½ cup shortening
2 eggs
3 cups flour
½ tsp. soda
1 tsp. cream of tartar
¼ tsp. nutmeg
1 Tbsp. water
1 tsp. vanilla

1. Cream sugar, butter, and shortening. Add eggs and beat until light and fluffy.
2. Sift and add dry ingredients. Add water and vanilla.
3. Divide dough in half and form two rolls. Chill overnight. Slice cookies ½ inch thick. Bake at 350° for 10-12 minutes.

Brown Sugar Cookies

2¼ cups brown sugar   Makes 9 dozen
1 cup margarine or shortening
3 eggs
1 tsp. soda
1 tsp. cinnamon
4 cups flour

1. Cream sugar and margarine. Add eggs and beat well.
2. Add soda, cinnamon, and flour. Mix well and chill for several hours.
3. Roll thinly on floured board and cut with cookie cutters. Bake at 350° for 7-8 minutes.

Molasses Cookies

1 cup shortening   Makes 8 dozen
½ lb. light brown sugar
1 pint dark baking molasses
1 pint buttermilk
6 cups flour
1 Tbsp. baking soda

1. Cream shortening and sugar. Add molasses and buttermilk.
2. Stir in flour and baking soda.
3. Drop in large dollops from teaspoon onto cookie sheet. Bake at 375° for 8-10 minutes.

Variation:
    Cookies may be glazed by brushing tops with egg yolk before baking.
    Add 1 tsp. ginger and 1 tsp. cinnamon with flour and soda.

Aunt Carrie's Butterscotch Ice-Box Cookies

Makes 7 dozen

1 cup butter
1 cup brown sugar
2 eggs
3½ cups flour
1 tsp. soda
1 tsp. cream of tartar
1 cup chopped dates
1 cup chopped nuts

1. Cream butter and sugar. Add eggs and beat well.
2. Sift dry ingredients together and gradually add to creamed mixture. Blend well. Stir in chopped dates and nuts.
3. Form into rolls on a platter. Cover and refrigerate overnight. Slice thin and bake at 400° for 8-10 minutes.

Short'nin' Bread Cookies

Makes 2½ dozen

4 cups flour (sifted)
dash of salt
1 cup brown sugar
2 cups butter

1. Combine flour, salt, and sugar. Mix well.
2. Cut in butter until mixture resembles fine crumbs. Work together by hand until dough forms a ball.
3. Pat or roll out ½ inch thick on lightly floured board. Cut circles with 2 inch cookie cutter. Bake at 350° for 20-25 minutes.

Sand Tarts

2 cups sugar
1 cup butter
2 eggs
4 cups flour

Makes 10 dozen

1 Cream sugar, butter, and eggs.
2. Blend in flour.
3. Roll dough very thin and cut in decorative shapes with cookie cutters. Brush top of cookies with egg white and sprinkle with colored sugar or crushed peanuts. Bake at 350° for 8-10 minutes.

Note:
Do not substitute other shortenings for butter.

from
Amish and Mennonite
kitchens

Drop Sugar Cookies

1½ cups sugar   Makes 5 dozen
1 cup margarine
2 eggs
1 cup buttermilk or sour cream
3¾ cups flour
2 tsp. baking powder
1 tsp. soda
1 tsp. vanilla

1. Cream sugar and shortening. Add eggs and beat well.
2. Add milk, dry ingredients, and vanilla and mix thoroughly.
3. Drop by teaspoons onto greased cookie sheet. Bake at 375° for 8-10 minutes.

Variation:
   Use 1 tsp. lemon extract in place of vanilla.
   Place a raisin in the center and sprinkle the top of each cookie with sugar before baking.

"Grandma always baked these to sell on market. I was glad when one broke in her box — she'd give it to me to eat!"

Fudge Nut Cookies

Makes 5½ dozen

1⅔ cup sugar
⅔ cup butter
2 eggs
1 cup cottage cheese
2 tsp. vanilla
2¾ cups flour
½ cup cocoa
1 tsp. baking powder
½ tsp. baking soda
½ tsp. salt
½ cup chopped nuts

1. Cream sugar, butter, eggs, and cottage cheese.
2. Add vanilla and dry ingredients. Stir in chopped nuts. Chill dough 2 hours.
3. Roll dough into balls the size of a walnut. Dip in granulated or powdered sugar. Place 2 inches apart on cookie sheet and bake at 350° for 8-10 minutes.

"Good and chocolate-y!"

Cookies

Fresh Glazed Apple Cookies

Makes 4½ dozen

1⅓ cup brown sugar
½ cup shortening
1 egg
2 cups flour
1 tsp. soda
½ tsp. salt
1 tsp. cinnamon
1 tsp. ground cloves
½ tsp. nutmeg
½ cup milk
1 cup apples (finely chopped, unpared)
1 cup raisins
1 cup nuts

1. Cream sugar and shortening. Add egg and beat well.
2. Add dry ingredients alternately with milk. Stir in apples, raisins, and nuts.
3. Drop by teaspoons onto cookie sheet. Bake at 350° for 12-15 minutes.

Glaze

1½ cups 10x sugar
2½ Tbsp. apple juice or milk
½ tsp. salt

¼ tsp. vanilla
1 Tbsp. butter

1. Cream butter. Gradually add sugar, juice or milk, salt, and vanilla. Beat until smooth.
2. Spread on top of Apple Cookies.

Walnut Supreme Cookies

Makes about 6 dozen

1 cup sugar
1 cup brown sugar
1 cup margarine
3 eggs
3½ cups flour
1 tsp. soda
2 tsp. baking powder
1 cup buttermilk
1 cup chopped walnuts

1. Cream sugars, shortening, and eggs.
2. Sift dry ingredients and add alternately with buttermilk. Fold in chopped nuts.
3. Drop by rounded teaspoons onto greased cookie sheet. Bake at 375° for 8-10 minutes.

Variation:
   After cooling cookies may be frosted with a butter frosting.

Golden Nuggets

Makes 4 dozen

½ cup sugar
¼ cup brown sugar
¾ cup shortening
1 egg
2 cups flour
1½ tsp. baking powder
½ tsp. salt
1 cup cooked, mashed carrots
1 tsp. vanilla
1 cup chopped walnuts

1. Cream sugars and shortening. Add egg, well beaten.
2. Sift dry ingredients together and add alternately with mashed carrots. Add vanilla. Stir in chopped walnuts.
3. Drop by rounded teaspoons onto greased cookie sheet. Bake at 400° for 8-10 minutes.
4. Frost with orange icing while warm.

Orange Icing

1 cup 10x sugar
2 tsp. grated orange rind
2 Tbsp. orange juice
Mix until smooth.

Applesauce Nuggets

Makes 3½ dozen

1 cup brown sugar
½ cup shortening
1 egg
1 cup applesauce
2 cups flour
½ tsp. salt
1 tsp. soda
½ tsp. cinnamon
¼ tsp. cloves
½ tsp. allspice
½ tsp. nutmeg
½ cup chopped pecans
1 cup butterscotch pieces

1. Cream sugar and shortening. Add egg and applesauce and beat well.
2. Sift together flour, salt, soda, and spices. Stir into creamed mixture.
3. Stir in chopped pecans and butterscotch pieces.
4. Drop by heaping teaspoons onto greased cookie sheet. Bake at 375° for 10-12 minutes.

Cookies

Boston Fruit Cookies

Makes 5 dozen

1½ cups brown sugar
1 cup shortening
3 eggs
3½ cups flour
pinch of salt
1 tsp. soda dissolved in
½ cup raisin juice
1 cup coconut
1 15 oz. box raisins (boiled, cooled, and drained)

1. Cream sugar and shortening. Add eggs and beat well.
2. Add flour, salt, and soda dissolved in raisin juice. Mix well.
3. Stir in coconut and raisins.
4. Drop by teaspoonfuls onto cookie sheet. Bake at 350° for 8-10 minutes.

Snowballs

Makes 4 dozen

1 cup soft butter
½ cup sifted 10x sugar
1 tsp. vanilla
2¼ cups sifted flour
¼ tsp. salt
¾ cup ground nuts, chilled

1. Cream together butter, sugar, and vanilla.
2. Add flour, salt, and nuts.
3. Roll into 1 inch balls.
4. Place on ungreased cookie sheet.
5. Bake at 400° for 10-12 minutes until set.
6. While still warm, roll in 10x sugar. Cool. Roll in sugar again.

Cookies

Cherry Winks

1 cup sugar   Makes 7 dozen
¾ cup shortening
2 eggs
2 Tbsp. milk
1 tsp. vanilla
1 cup chopped nuts
1 cup chopped dates
2¼ cups flour
1 tsp. baking powder
½ tsp. salt
½ tsp. soda

1. Cream shortening and sugar. Add eggs, milk, vanilla, nuts, and dates.
2. Sift and add dry ingredients.
3. Form balls the size of a walnut. Roll in crushed corn flakes. Flatten slightly and top with half of a maraschino cherry. Bake at 375° for 10-12 minutes.

Pecan Tassies (Tiny Pecan Pies)

½ cup butter or margarine Makes 2 dozen
3 oz. cream cheese
1 cup flour
¾ cup brown sugar
1 egg
1 Tbsp. butter or margarine
1 tsp. vanilla
dash of salt
⅔ cup pecans, coarsely broken

1. Blend together softened butter or margarine and cream cheese. Stir in flour. Chill dough about 1 hour.
2. Shape dough into 2 dozen 1 inch balls. Place in ungreased 1¾ inch muffin pans. Press dough evenly against sides and bottom of each muffin cup.
3. Blend together brown sugar, egg, butter or margarine, vanilla, and salt. Beat just until smooth.
4. Divide half of the pecans among pastry lined muffin cups. Add egg mixture and top with remaining pecans. Bake at 325° for 25 minutes or until filling is set.
5. Cool before removing from pans.

Soft Raisin Cookies

Makes about 9 dozen

2 cups raisins
1 cup boiling water
¾ cup shortening
2 cups sugar
3 eggs
1 tsp. vanilla
4 cups flour
1 tsp. baking powder
1 tsp. baking soda
1 tsp. salt
1 tsp. cinnamon
¼ tsp. cloves
¼ tsp. nutmeg
1 cup chopped nuts

1. Add boiling water to raisins. Cook 5 minutes. Set aside to cool.
2. Cream shortening and sugar. Add eggs and vanilla and beat well.
3. Sift together flour, baking powder, baking soda, salt, and spices. Add alternately with raisin liquid to creamed mixture. Stir in raisins and nuts.
4. Chill dough for several hours or overnight.
5. Drop by teaspoons onto greased cookie sheet. Bake at 350° for about 12 minutes.

Cookies

Desserts

from
Amish and Mennonite
kitchens

from
Amish and Mennonite
kitchens

Desserts

Lighten up a meal with apple strudel or sunbeam tapioca! A refreshing dessert can be the right finish to any dinner. Sometimes graham cracker pudding. Sometimes apricot sponge.

No child will turn down cherry delight or homemade ice cream! What's more nostalgic than bread pudding or egg custard?

These desserts need no pie or cake back-up. They stand well on their own — from sturdy apple dumplings and peach longcake (nearly meals in themselves) to fluffy Spanish cream or chewy rhubarb crunch.

Most of these dishes also travel well. Cottage cheese cake has been to many family reunions. Amish date pudding will bless any covered dish social!

Amish Date Pudding

1 cup dates, chopped
1 cup boiling water
1 tsp. baking soda
1 cup sugar
1 egg, beaten
3 Tbsp. butter, melted
1 cup flour
1 tsp. vanilla
½ cup nuts, chopped
3 cups sweetened whipped cream
3 bananas, sliced

Makes about
18 servings

1.   Combine dates, water, and soda. Mix well and let cool.
2.   Add remaining ingredients except cream and bananas and mix well.
3.   Pour batter into a greased, waxed paper lined 9"x13" pan. Bake at 350° for 30~40 minutes.
4.   Allow cake to cool. To serve, crumble cake slightly. Fold with whipped cream and sliced bananas.

Apple Strudel

1½ cup flour   Makes 9-12 servings
½ cup sugar
⅛ tsp. salt
½ cup butter or margarine
5 cups apples, peeled and sliced
½ cup sugar
3 Tbsp. tapioca
⅔ tsp. cinnamon

1. Cut flour, ½ cup sugar, salt, and margarine together with two knives or a pastry cutter. Reserve ¾ cup crumb mixture for topping.
2. Press remaining crumb mixture on bottom and sides of 8" or 9" square pan.
3. Mix apples, ½ cup sugar, tapioca, and cinnamon and spread over crust.
4. Bake at 425° for 20 minutes. Sprinkle reserved crumbs on top and bake 20 minutes more.
5. Serve warm or cold with whipped cream or ice cream.

Apple Dumplings

Makes 8 servings

- 8 apples, cored and pared
- 3 cups flour
- 1 tsp. salt
- 1¼ cup shortening
- 1 egg, beaten
- ⅓ cup cold water
- 1 Tbsp. vinegar
- ½ cup margarine
- 1 cup brown sugar
- 4 Tbsp. water

1. Mix flour and salt. Cut in shortening.
2. Combine egg, ⅓ cup cold water, and vinegar and stir into the shortening mixture. Let stand a few minutes.
3. Roll out dough on a floured board and cut into squares, so that each is large enough to fit up around each apple. When an apple is completely wrapped in dough, place it in a greased 9"x13" baking pan.
4. Bring margarine, brown sugar, and 4 Tbsp. water to a boil. Pour over dumplings.
5. Bake at 350° for 40~50 minutes or until dumplings are golden brown.

Desserts

Fruit Cobbler

Makes 8 servings

1¼ cups flour, sifted
1½ tsp. baking powder
½ tsp. salt
½ cup sugar
½ cup milk
2 Tbsp. shortening, melted
1¾ cup fruit
2 cups hot water or fruit juice
¾ cup sugar
2 Tbsp. margarine

1. Sift flour, baking powder, salt, and ½ cup sugar together. Add milk and shortening and stir only until smooth.
2. Spread dough evenly in greased shallow pan (about 12"x 8"). Arrange fruit over top.
3. Combine hot water or juice, ¾ cup sugar, and margarine in a saucepan and bring to a boil. Pour over fruit.
4. Bake immediately at 375° for 45~50 minutes. Serve warm.

Note:
Blueberries, peaches, cherries, or raspberries all work well in this cobbler.

Cherry Delight

2 cups graham
    cracker crumbs
½ cup butter
1 8 oz. package cream cheese, softened
2 cups whipped cream
¾ cup sugar
4½ Tbsp. cornstarch
3 cups water
2 cups cherries

Makes about
15 servings

1. Combine cracker crumbs and butter. Mix until crumbly. Reserve 1 cup for topping. Pat crumbs into 9"x13" pan. Bake at 350° for 5 minutes. Cool.
2. Beat cream cheese until fluffy. Add whipped cream. Spread mixture over crumb crust.
3. Combine sugar, cornstarch, and water. Cook over medium heat, stirring constantly, until mixture is thick and clear. Remove from heat. Stir in fruit. Spread fruit mixture over cream cheese. Sprinkle with reserved crumbs. Chill several hours before serving.

Desserts

from
Amish and Mennonite
kitchens

Rhubarb Crunch

1 cup flour, sifted   Makes 6-8 servings
    (½ white; ½ whole wheat)
¼ cup oatmeal, uncooked
1 cup brown sugar, packed
½ cup butter, melted
1 tsp. cinnamon
1 cup sugar
2 Tbsp. cornstarch
1 cup water
1 tsp. vanilla
2 cups rhubarb, diced

1. Stir together flour, oatmeal, brown sugar, butter, and cinnamon until crumbly. Set aside half of crumbs. Pat remaining crumbs over bottom of 9" square baking pan.
2. Combine sugar, cornstarch, water, and vanilla, stirring until smooth. Add rhubarb and cook until mixture becomes thick and clear.
3. Pour rhubarb sauce over crumbs. Crumble remaining crumbs over top sauce.
4. Bake at 350° for 1 hour.

Variation:
Use cherries or blueberries instead of rhubarb.

Fruit Upside-down Pudding

Makes 8 servings

2 cups brown sugar
4 eggs
3 Tbsp. hot water
1 cup flour
1 tsp. baking powder
½ tsp. vanilla
3 Tbsp. butter
2 cups fruit, any kind

1. Combine 1 cup brown sugar and eggs. Beat well. Add water and beat again. Add flour, baking powder, and vanilla and mix well.
2. Combine remaining brown sugar and butter in heavy saucepan. Heat until sugar is melted. Pour caramel mixture into bottom of a 9"x9" cake pan. Add fruit. Spread batter over fruit. Bake at 350° for 30 minutes. Remove from oven and immediately turn pan upside down onto a serving platter. Serve warm with milk.

Peach Long Cake

Makes 10 servings

4 cups peaches,
    sliced
½ cup sugar

Dough

2 cups flour
4 tsp. baking powder
6 Tbsp. sugar
¾ tsp. salt
⅓ cup shortening
1 large egg, beaten
⅔ cup milk

1. Sprinkle sugar over sliced peaches. Set aside.
2. Sift flour. Add baking powder, sugar, and salt. Cut in shortening. Add egg and milk and stir until moistened. Spread dough into a well-greased 9" x 13" pan. Arrange peach slices over dough.

Topping

¼ cup margarine
¼ cup sugar
3 Tbsp. flour

1. Cream together all ingredients. Drop by spoonfuls over peaches.
2. Bake at 375° for 30 minutes. Serve warm with milk or whipped cream.

Apricot Sponge

1 lb. dried apricots
1 pkg. unflavored gelatin
   dissolved in ¼ cup cold water
2 cups apricot juice
1 cup sugar
juice of ½ lemon
2 egg whites
whipped cream

Makes about
12 servings

1. Place apricots in heavy saucepan and cover with water. Cook until soft. Drain apricots reserving juice. Add hot water to make 2 cups juice.
2. Mash apricots through vegetable press. Combine apricot pulp and juice, gelatin, sugar, and lemon juice in large mixing bowl. Beat until cold. Fold in slightly beaten egg whites. Pour into mold or serving dish. Chill. Serve with whipped cream.

Creamy Rice Pudding

Makes 10 servings

1 quart milk
½ cup rice
2 Tbsp. butter
¼ cup sugar
¼ tsp. salt
2 eggs
1 tsp. vanilla

1. Stir together milk, rice, butter, sugar, and salt. Pour into double boiler and cook slowly for 1-1½ hours until rice is soft.
2. Beat the eggs. Remove 1 cup hot milk and rice from double boiler and gradually add to the beaten eggs. Then add the egg mixture to the rest of the pudding. Stir in the vanilla. Serve either warm or cold.

Variations:

1. Add ¼-½ tsp. nutmeg to rice mixture before cooking.

2. After pudding cools, fold in ½ cup crushed pineapple or ½ cup banana slices, and 1 cup whipped cream.

Old-Fashioned Bread Pudding

Makes 10 servings

5 slices bread, at
   least 3 days old
1 cup raisins, optional
3 cups milk
⅓ cup sugar
pinch of salt
3 eggs, slightly beaten
¼ tsp. cinnamon
2 Tbsp. sugar

1. Toast bread lightly, butter generously, then break into pieces, about ¼" square. Arrange in buttered 9"x9" baking dish. Sprinkle with raisins.
2. Scald the milk. Stir in sugar and salt. Pour over eggs and blend thoroughly.
3. Pour over bread and stir so the bread is completely wet. Combine cinnamon and sugar and sprinkle over top.
4. Set baking dish in pan of hot water. Bake at 350° for 1 hour or until a knife, inserted in the center of the pudding, comes out clean. Serve hot or cold.

Desserts

from
Amish and Mennonite
kitchens

Egg Custard

4 eggs
½ cup sugar
¼ tsp. salt
1 tsp. vanilla
4 cups scalded milk

Makes about
7 servings

1. Combine all ingredients in blender and mix thoroughly. Pour into custard cups. Set cups in shallow baking pan and add hot water to cover all but ½" of the custard cups. Bake at 475° for 5 minutes and then 425° for 15-20 minutes or until set. Cool before serving.

Variations:
1. Sprinkle custards with nutmeg before baking.
2. Add ¾ cup coconut to custards before baking.
3. Add 2 cups mashed, cooked pumpkin, ½ tsp. ginger, 1 tsp. cinnamon, ½ tsp. cloves, ¼ tsp. nutmeg, and ¼ tsp. salt to custards before baking.

Cracker Pudding

2 eggs, separated   Makes 6-8 servings
⅔ cup sugar
1 quart milk
1¼-1½ cups saltine crackers,
    coarsely broken
¾ cup coconut, grated (optional)
1 tsp. vanilla
3 Tbsp. sugar

1. Beat egg yolks and sugar together. Pour into saucepan and heat. Gradually add the milk, stirring constantly.
2. Add crackers and coconut and cook until thickened. Remove from heat and stir in vanilla.
3. Pour into baking dish. Add 3 Tbsp. sugar to egg whites and beat untill stiffened. Spread over pudding, then brown the meringue under the broiler.

"This is very easy and quick to make~ and has a good consistency."

from
Amish and Mennonite kitchens

Graham Cracker Pudding

16 whole Graham crackers	Makes about 9 servings
¼ cup sugar	
¼ cup butter	
4 tsp. flour	
½ cup plus 2 Tbsp. sugar	
2 cups milk	
3 eggs, separated	
½ tsp. vanilla	
1 cup shredded coconut	

1. Crush graham crackers. Combine with ¼ cup sugar and butter. Mix to form fine crumbs. Press ¾ of crumb mixture into bottom and sides of baking dish. Reserve remaining crumbs.

2. Combine flour and ½ cup sugar in top of double boiler. Add milk. Heat to boiling. Beat egg yolks and combine with ½ cup hot milk mixture. Pour this into remaining hot milk and heat to boiling again. Boil 2-3 minutes, stirring constantly. Remove from heat and add vanilla and coconut. Pour into cracker-lined dish.

3. Beat egg whites until stiff. Gradually add remaining 2 Tbsp. sugar. Pile beaten egg whites on top of pudding. Sprinkle with reserved cracker crumbs. Bake at 350° for 5-8 minutes until meringue is browned. Cool before serving.

Sunbeam Tapioca

½ cup sugar   Makes 6 servings
¼ cup quick cooking tapioca
½ tsp. salt
½ cup pineapple juice
1 cup water
½ cup orange juice
1½ Tbsp. lemon juice
½ cup diced orange sections
1 cup crushed pineapple, drained

1. In heavy saucepan combine sugar, tapioca, salt, pineapple juice, and water. Bring to a boil. Boil 3-5 minutes until thickened. Cool.
2. Stir in remaining ingredients. Chill. Serve with whipped cream.

from
Amish and Mennonite
kitchens

Tapioca Pudding

4 cups milk
⅓ cup minute tapioca
2 eggs, separated
½ cup sugar
pinch of salt
½ tsp. vanilla or lemon extract

Makes about
10 servings

1. Combine milk and tapioca in heavy saucepan. Cook, stirring constantly, until tapioca is clear.
2. Beat egg yolks with sugar and salt. Add ½ cup hot milk mixture to egg yolks. Return this to remaining hot milk. Heat again to boiling point. Boil 2 minutes, stirring constantly. Remove from heat. Fold in stiffly beaten egg whites and flavoring. Pour into serving dish.

Variation:
1. Substitute ¼ cup honey in place of sugar.
2. Use 3 cups grape juice and 1 cup milk instead of 4 cups milk.

Spanish Cream

1 envelope unflavored gelatin
2 Tbsp. sugar
⅛ tsp. salt
2 eggs, separated
2 cups milk
1 tsp. vanilla
4 Tbsp. sugar

Makes 6-8 servings

1. Mix gelatin, 2 Tbsp. sugar, and salt thoroughly in top of double boiler.
2. Beat egg yolks and milk together and add to gelatin. Cook over boiling water, about 5 minutes, until gelatin dissolves.
3. Remove from heat and stir in the vanilla.
4. Beat egg whites until stiff, adding the 4 Tbsp. sugar while beating.
5. Fold stiff whites into pudding. Pour in serving dish and chill until set. (The pudding will separate into 2 layers.) Serve topped with whipped cream.

Desserts

Vanilla Pudding

Makes 18~20 servings

1 cup milk
2 cups sugar
4 eggs, beaten
3 rounded Tbsp. cornstarch
1 rounded Tbsp. flour
pinch of salt
2 Tbsp. vanilla
1¾ quarts milk

1. Mix together 1 cup milk, sugar, eggs, cornstarch, flour, and salt until smooth.
2. Add to remaining milk and vanilla. Slowly heat to the boiling point.
3. Remove from heat and cool.

Cottage Steam Pudding

Makes 8 servings

1 cup sugar
3 Tbsp. butter, melted
1 egg
2 cups flour
1 tsp. soda
2 tsp. cream of tartar
1 cup milk
1 cup raisins or other fruit

1. Cream sugar and butter. Add egg and beat well. Add dry ingredients and milk. Beat thoroughly. Stir in fruit.
2. Place in double boiler. Steam 1½-1¾ hours. Do not lift lid any time during steaming. Remove from kettle onto serving platter. Serve warm with milk.

Grapenut Pudding

1 Tbsp. margarine, melted   Makes 6 servings

½ cup sugar

2 egg yolks

1½ cups milk

½ cup raisins

¾ cup grapenuts

2 egg whites

1 tsp. vanilla

1. Mix together the margarine, sugar, egg yolks, milk, raisins, and grapenuts.
2. Pour into a greased casserole and bake at 350° for 45 minutes or until browned.
3. Beat egg whites until soft peaks form. Fold into pudding along with vanilla.
4. Cool. Serve with a dollop of whipped cream.

Snow Pudding

Makes 6 servings

1 cup water
6 Tbsp. sugar
3½ Tbsp. cornstarch
2 egg whites
1 tsp. vanilla
1½ cup milk
2 egg yolks, beaten

1. Combine water, 3 Tbsp. sugar, and 2 Tbsp. cornstarch in heavy saucepan. Cook until thickened.
2. Beat egg whites until stiff. Stir into hot cornstarch mixture. Add ½ tsp. vanilla. Pour mixture into serving dish.
3. Combine milk, egg yolks, remaining sugar, cornstarch, and vanilla. Cook over medium heat until thickened. Pour over first layer in serving dish. Cool. Serve with whipped cream if desired.

Frozen Pumpkin Parfait Squares

Makes 9-12 servings

1½ cups graham
    cracker crumbs
¼ cup butter or margarine, melted

¼ cup sugar
½ cup pecans, finely chopped
1 qt. vanilla ice cream
1½ cup pumpkin, mashed
½ cup brown sugar
½ tsp. salt
1 tsp. cinnamon
¼ tsp. ginger
⅓ tsp. ground cloves
whipping cream
chopped pecans

1. Combine crumbs, butter, sugar, and chopped nuts. Press mixture firmly against bottom and sides of 9" square pan. Bake at 375° for 8 minutes. Cool.
2. Allow ice cream to soften until it becomes custardy. Stir in pumpkin, brown sugar, and spices.
3. Pile into cooled crust. Place in freezer until hard. Cover with foil to store.
4. Take from freezer 20 minutes before serving; then cut into squares.
5. Dollop with whipped cream and sprinkle with chopped nuts.

Desserts

Scotch Refrigerator Dish

3 Tbsp. margarine   Makes 12 servings
1 cup light brown sugar
¼ cup flour
1½ cups milk
2 eggs, separated
1 box vanilla wafers, crushed
1 cup pecans, coarsely chopped

1. Melt margarine over water in top of double boiler. Mix brown sugar and flour and add to melted margarine. Blend well.
2. Add milk slowly. Cook over hot water, stirring constantly until it becomes thick and smooth. Cook 15 minutes longer.
3. Slowly add slightly beaten egg yolks. Cook for 2 minutes. Remove from heat and gently fold in stiffly beaten egg whites.
4. Cover bottom of 9"x 9" baking pan with ½ of cookie crumbs. Cover with ½ of cooked filling. Top with ⅓ of cookie crumbs and ½ the pecans. Pour in remaining filling. Top with rest of cookie crumbs and pecans. Chill several hours. Top with whipped cream to serve.

Zucchini Bars

¾ cup butter or margarine	Makes about 2 doz. bars
½ cup brown sugar	
½ cup granulated sugar	
2 eggs	
1 tsp. vanilla	
1¾ cup flour	
1½ tsp. baking powder	
1 cup shredded coconut	
2 cups shredded zucchini	
½ cup nuts, chopped	

1. Beat butter until light and fluffy. Gradually beat in sugar. Add eggs and beat well. Add vanilla.

2. Sift together flour and baking powder. Stir into egg mixture. Stir in zucchini, coconut, and nuts. Spread evenly in well greased 10"x 15"x 1½" pan. Bake at 350° for 40 minutes. Cool. Cut in bars.

Variation:
    Frost with butter cream frosting flavored with a bit of cinnamon and vanilla.

Desserts

from
Amish and Mennonite
kitchens

Peanut Butter Bars

¼ cup butter or margarine, melted   Makes 48 bars
1¼ cups flour
½ cup brown sugar
1 cup peanut butter
6 oz. chocolate bits
3 Tbsp. water

1. Blend butter, flour, and sugar and press into a 13"x 9"x 2" baking pan. Bake 20 minutes at 350°.
2. Spread peanut butter over above mixture. Cool.
3. Melt chocolate bits and water. Spread over peanut butter. Cool. Cut into bars.

Hello Dollies

¼ cup butter or margarine   Makes about 2 dozen squares
1 cup graham cracker crumbs
1 cup coconut
1 cup chocolate bits
1 cup pecans, chopped
1 can sweetened condensed milk

1. Spread softened butter on bottom of a 9" x 9" baking pan.
2. Add cracker crumbs, then coconut, then chocolate bits, then pecans. Pour milk over all. Bake at 325° for 30 minutes. Cool and cut in squares.

Butterscotch Bars

½ cup butter or margarine
2 cups brown sugar
2 cups flour
1 tsp. salt
2 tsp. baking powder
2 eggs
1 tsp. vanilla
1 cup peanuts, chopped

Makes 1 long cake pan

1. Melt butter, then stir in brown sugar, and set aside to cool.
2. Mix together the flour, salt, and baking powder.
3. Stir eggs into cooled brown sugar mixture, then blend in dry ingredients, vanilla, and peanuts.
4. Spread in a greased 9" x 13" cake pan. Bake at 350° for 30 minutes.

Cottage Cheese Cake

Makes 9-12 servings

1½ cups cornflakes, finely crushed
¼ cup sugar
1 tsp. cinnamon
¼ tsp. nutmeg
¼ cup margarine or butter, melted
¾ cup sugar
2 envelopes (2 Tbsp) unflavored gelatin
¼ tsp. salt
2 egg yolks, beaten
1 6 oz. can (¾ cup) evaporated milk
1 tsp. lemon peel, grated
24 oz. cottage cheese, sieved or blended
1 Tbsp. lemon juice
1½ tsp. vanilla
2 egg whites
¼ cup sugar
½ to 1 cup whipped cream

1. Combine cornflakes, ¼ cup sugar, cinnamon, nutmeg, and margarine to form crust. Reserve ⅓ of mixture. Press remaining crumbs on bottom of 9" square baking pan. Chill.
2. In double boiler combine ¾ cup sugar, gelatin, and salt. Stir in egg yolks and

milk.   Cook over simmering water, stirring until gelatin dissolves and mixture thickens. Remove from heat.

3. Stir lemon peel, cottage cheese, lemon juice, and vanilla into gelatin mixture. Chill until partially congealed and custardy.

4. Beat egg whites until soft peaks form. Gradually add ¼ cup sugar and beat until stiff peaks form. Fold into gelatin mixture.

5. Fold in whipped cream. Pour over corn-flake crust. Sprinkle with remaining crumbs and chill.

"This cake works well any time. It looks cool for summer and snowy white for winter holidays."

Ice Cream

3 eggs, beaten   Makes 4 quarts
2 cups sugar
3 cups cream
2 tsp. vanilla
dash of salt
1 quart fruit, chopped

1. Mix all ingredients together thoroughly.
Pour into 4 quart freezer container,
adding additional fruit or cream if
necessary to make container ⅔ full.
2. Turn freezer until firm.

"We make this on family evenings after
the work is done, or on any other occasion
we can come up with!"

Plum Kuchen

Makes about 30 bars

½ cup sugar
1 cup butter or margarine
2 eggs
¼ tsp. cinnamon
⅛ tsp. cloves
1½ tsp. almond extract
½ Tbsp. lemon juice
2½ cups flour
1½ tsp. baking powder
½ cup ground almonds
2 lbs. plums (or apples or peaches)
    quartered
brown sugar
cinnamon
butter

1. Cream together sugar and butter. Add eggs and beat well. Stir in cinnamon, cloves, extract, and lemon juice.
2. Sift together flour and baking powder. Stir into sugar mixture. Stir in almonds. Chill dough for 1 hour. Press into a 9"x 13" baking pan or cookie sheet. Arrange fruit over dough in rows. Sprinkle with brown sugar and cinnamon. Dot with butter. Bake at 375° for 35 minutes.

Desserts

Jams
Jellies and Relishes

from
Amish and Mennonite
kitchens

Jams, Jellies, and Relishes

An overabundant garden or fruit tree need not be a problem.

Instead, either may be an excuse to get out the jars to make jelly. Or a reason to dust off the stockpot to do up some ketchup or sweet pickles.

When bread is a part of every meal, jams and jellies become a must. And a pleasure. (They are also a happy solution for any cook grieved by overripe fruit or vegetables.)

What's more, heavy meals can be lightly offset with the pungent addition of pickled beets or watermelon rind.

And what better farewell to the garden is there than chow chow, that colorful and tempting combination of last season's vegetables, all preserved for year-around eating!

Deviled Eggs

6 eggs　　　　　　　　　Makes 12 halves
2 Tbsp. commercial mayonnaise
2 Tbsp. homemade mayonnaise
½ tsp. prepared mustard
salt to taste

1. Hard-boil eggs. Cool, peel, and cut in half. Remove yolks from whites.
2. Mash yolks. Mix yolks with remaining ingredients. Fill egg whites with yolk mixture. Garnish with paprika and stuffed olive slices if desired.

Mayonnaise

1 egg　　　　　　　　　Makes about
1 cup sugar　　　　　　2 cups
1 Tbsp. flour
1 cup water
½ cup vinegar

Combine egg, sugar, and flour. Add enough of the water to make a smooth paste. Add remaining water and vinegar and bring to a boil, stirring constantly. Cook until thickened.

Jams
Jellies and Relishes

from
Amish and Mennonite
kitchens

Homemade Apple Butter

40 gallons apple cider   Makes 25 gallons
40 bushels apples
40 lbs. sugar

1. Heat cider to boiling at 5:30 a.m.
2. Peel, core, and slice apples. At 2:30 p.m. add ⅓ of the apple slices. After this addition the mixture must be stirred constantly.
3. At 3:30 p.m. add another ⅓ of the apples. Add sugar gradually.
4. At 4:30 p.m. add the remaining apples.
5. Continue stirring mixture until about 8:00 p.m. or until apple butter is thickened. Pour into jars and seal.

"We've actually tried this and it's delicious!"

Unstirred Apple Butter

    5 gallons apples
    10 lbs. sugar
    1 tsp. cinnamon
    ¼ tsp. cloves
    1 cup vinegar

1. Wash, core, and slice (do not peel) apples. Place apples, sugar, and spices in a large kettle. Cover tightly and cook overnight over low heat. Do not lift lid.
2. In the morning add 1 cup vinegar. Simmer 6 hours over low heat without removing lid.
3. Put apples through a food sieve. Put into jars and seal.

Variation:
    1. Cut all ingredients in half and place altogether in 6 qt. crock pot. Boil 6 hours. Put through food sieve. Put into jars and seal.

Apple Butter in the Oven

8 qts. thick applesauce
8 qts. fresh cider
4 cups sugar
1 tsp. salt

1. Make 8 quarts of thick applesauce. Place hot applesauce into the oven at 400°.
2. Place cider in large kettle and boil until half has evaporated. Add cider to sauce in the oven. Allow oven door to stand slightly ajar so steam can escape. Stir occasionally.
3. After about 2 hours add sugar and salt. Mix well. Allow about 2 more hours of cooking time until apple butter is the desired consistency, remembering to stir occasionally. Seal in jars.

"Each fall in the past we boiled apple butter in a large copper kettle, then put it into crocks. I still get hungry for that kind of apple butter. I believe the only way to get that flavor is to boil down the cider. So by experimenting I've come up with this method."

Pear Butter

    6 quarts pear sauce
    1 quart apple cider
    ¼ tsp. cinnamon
    3 lbs. brown sugar

1. To make pear sauce, wash, core, and peel pears. Cut into quarters. Add a little water and cook until soft and mushy.
2. Mix pear sauce with cider, cinnamon, and brown sugar in large roaster. Place in a 400° oven for 3-4 hours. Stir occasionally during baking time. Allow oven door to stand a bit ajar so moisture can escape. This will boil down to about ½ volume. Put in jars and seal.

    "This makes more spreadings using less sugar!"

from
Amish and Mennonite
kitchens

Pear and Apricot Butter

5 lbs. pears, peeled and cored
1 lb. dried apricots
3 lbs. sugar

Combine pears and apricots with just enough water to cook until soft. Put fruit through food press. Add sugar and cook until thickened, stirring often. Pour into jars and seal.

Grape Jelly

1 lb. grapes
1 lb. sugar
3 Tbsp. water

Combine all ingredients. Boil for 20 minutes. Put through food press. Pour into jars and seal.

Peach Pineapple Preserves

7 cups ripe peaches, chopped or mashed
1~20 oz. can crushed pineapple, drained
5 cups sugar
1 6 oz. box peach jello

Combine peaches, pineapple, and sugar. Cook over low heat for 15 minutes, stirring occasionally. Remove from heat and add jello. Mix well. Pour into jars and seal.

Pineapple Jam

1 20 oz. can crushed pineapple and
    liquid
2 cups sugar
1 cup white Karo syrup

Cook pineapple and sugar together for 20 minutes. Add Karo syrup and heat to boiling point. Pour into jars and seal.

Jams
Jellies and Relishes

Fruit Jam

3 cups pears, grated
3 cups peaches, grated
2 cups crushed pineapple
8 cups sugar
1 6 oz. package Orange jello

1. Combine fruits and sugar. Allow to come to a full boil. Boil 20 minutes.
2. Add jello and stir until dissolved. Pour into jars and seal.

Strawberry Jam

6 cups sugar
1 cup water
2 cups strawberries, crushed
1 tsp. alum

1. Combine sugar and water. Boil 10 minutes.
2. Add strawberries and boil 5 minutes longer.
3. Add alum and boil 1 more minute. Pour into jars and seal.

Variation:
For a thinner consistency, use only 4 cups sugar.

Rhubarb Jelly

5 cups rhubarb, diced
4 cups sugar
1 6 oz. box strawberry jello

Combine rhubarb and sugar. Let stand overnight. In the morning, cook rhubarb for 5 minutes. Remove from heat and stir in jello. Pour into jars and seal.

Variation:
Add 1 20 oz. can crushed pineapple.

Peach Marmalade

5 cups peaches, mashed
2 cups apricots, mashed
7 cups sugar
1 6 oz. package Orange jello

1. Combine fruit and sugar. Cook 15 minutes.
2. Add jello. Cook until jello is dissolved.
3. Pour into jars and seal.

Jams
Jellies and Relishes

Marmalade

2 oranges
1 grapefruit
kumquats (enough to make 1½ cups
when seeded and ground)
sugar

1. Peel and chop oranges and grapefruit. Add kumquats. Add as much sugar as the quantity of combined fruit.
2. Cook mixture over medium heat until thickened. Pour into jars and seal.

Quince Honey

2 cups quince, grated
2 cups apples, grated
2 cups water
6 cups sugar

Combine fruits and water. Bring to a boil. Add sugar gradually and stir until all sugar is dissolved. Cook slowly until fruit is clear and mixture is thickened, about 20 minutes. Pour into jars and seal.

Bread and Butter Pickles

Makes 4 quarts

- 4 qts. cucumbers, thinly sliced
- 3 medium onions, thinly sliced
- 2 peppers, chopped
- ½ cup salt
- ice cubes

Syrup

- 3 cups vinegar
- 5 cups sugar
- ½ tsp. turmeric
- ½ tsp. celery seed
- 2 Tbsp. mustard seed

1. Combine cucumbers, onions, peppers, and salt. Cover with ice cubes and let stand for 3 hours. Drain well.
2. Combine all syrup ingredients in large kettle. Add pickle mixture. Bring to a boil. Place in jars and seal.

Jams
Jellies and Relishes

Nine Day Sweet Pickles

100 medium size pickles
horseradish leaves
1 Tbsp. alum
4 cups water
4 cups vinegar
6 lbs. sugar
1 Tbsp. nutmeg
4 sticks cinnamon

1. Wash pickles. Soak in 1 gallon water and 1 cup salt for 5 days.
2. Drain and cover with boiling water for 24 hours.
3. Drain. Cut pickles lengthwise. Place pickles in crock alternating layers of pickles with horseradish leaves. Add alum. Pour boiling water over pickles until covered. Let stand overnight.
4. Drain pickles. Remove leaves. Cover pickles with boiling water. Let stand for 3 hours. Drain.
5. Combine water, vinegar, and sugar. Tie spices in a bag and add to liquid. Heat to boiling and pour over pickles. Drain and heat syrup once a day for 3 days pouring over pickles each time.

6. On the 9th day, drain syrup and pack pickles into jars. Heat syrup. Pour over pickles and seal.

Note:

Syrup amount may need to be doubled to cover pickles. Seal leftover syrup in jars to use the following year.

"This was my Grandmother's recipe.
"Sometimes I use the leftover syrup in ham salad. You can also grind some of the pickles and mix them into the salad."

Jams
Jellies and Relishes

from
Amish and Mennonite
kitchens

Freezer Pickles

7 cups cucumbers, thinly sliced
1 cup onions, thinly sliced
1 cup peppers, thinly sliced
2 tsp. salt
½ tsp. celery seed
2 cups sugar
1 cup vinegar

1. Combine all ingredients and mix well. Place in covered container and refrigerate for 3 days. Stir each day.
2. After 3 days, put in containers in freezer.

"These are just delicious pickles!"

Dill Pickles

about 7 lbs.   Makes 7 quarts
    medium cucumbers
fresh dill
garlic cloves
4 cups vinegar
3 qts. water
2 Tbsp. sugar
¾ cup salt

1. Cut cucumbers into long spears and pack into quart jars. Place a fresh dill sprig and 1 garlic clove in each jar.
2. Combine vinegar, water, sugar, salt, and boil with 2 heads dill for 2 minutes. Pour syrup over pickles in jars. Seal jars and boil in canner for 10 minutes.

"If I have to choose one kind of pickle to make in a summer, I'll choose these!"

Jams
Jellies and Relishes

Green Tomato Relish

24 green tomatoes
4 red peppers
2 yellow peppers
12 onions
4 cups sugar
4 cups vinegar
4 Tbsp. salt
6 Tbsp. celery seed
1 Tbsp. turmeric

1. Grind tomatoes, peppers, and onions. Drain overnight.
2. Combine vegetables and all other ingredients. Bring to a boil and cook for 15 minutes. Pour into jars and seal.

"I like to make this relish because my children all tell me it's the best relish around! I also like to take a jar of it as a gift for our hostess when we're invited out to eat."

Pepper Relish

8 large onions	Makes about
1 medium head cabbage	8 pints
10 green tomatoes	
12 green peppers	
6 red sweet peppers	
½ cup salt	
6 cups sugar	
1 Tbsp. mustard seed	
1 Tbsp. celery seed	
1½ tsp. turmeric	
4 cups vinegar	

Grind onions, cabbage, tomatoes, and peppers. Add remaining ingredients and mix well. Bring to a boil. Pour into jars and seal.

Variation:

Grind vegetables. Add 3 Tbsp. salt, 1 cup vinegar, 3 cups sugar, and 2 cups prepared mustard. Mix well and cook for 15 minutes, stirring constantly. Add 2 Tbsp. cornstarch and mix well. Remove from heat and stir in 1 quart mayonnaise. Pour into jars and seal.

Jams
Jellies and Relishes

from
Amish and Mennonite
kitchens

Pickled Peppers

3 lb. green, red, and yellow peppers
2½ cups white vinegar
2½ cups water
1¼ cups sugar
8 cloves garlic
2 tsp. salt

Makes 8 half-pints

1. Combine vinegar, water, and sugar. Heat to boiling.
2. Wash peppers. Cut into ½" strips. Place pepper strips in bowl and add enough boiling water to cover peppers. Cover bowl and let stand exactly 5 minutes. Drain.
3. Pack peppers into jars. Place 1 garlic clove and ¼ tsp. salt in each jar. Pour hot liquid over peppers and seal.

Pickled Red Beets

- 20 medium size red beets
- 2½ cups vinegar
- 2½ cups beet juice
- 1 cup sugar
- 2 tsp. salt
- 10 whole cloves
- 2 cinnamon sticks

1. Scrub beets and remove tops. Cook beets until tender. Drain and reserve beet juice. Remove skins and cut beets into chunks.
2. Combine vinegar, juice, sugar, and spices. Bring to a boil. Remove spices. Add beet chunks and boil again. Pour into jars and seal.

Red Beet Eggs

- 6 hard-boiled eggs, peeled
- 2½ cups leftover red beet juice syrup

Pour cool syrup over cooked and peeled eggs. Let stand overnight. To serve, slice the eggs in half, lengthwise.

Jams
Jellies and Relishes

353

Pickled Watermelon Rind

5 lbs. watermelon rind   Makes 6 pints
2½ lbs. sugar
2 cups vinegar
2 cups water
½ tsp. oil of cloves
½ tsp. oil of cinnamon

1. Pare watermelon rind and cut in 2" pieces. Mix ½ cup salt with 2 quarts water and soak rind overnight. Drain and rinse well. Drain again. Cook rind in fresh water until tender. Drain.

2. Combine vinegar, water, and spices. Bring to a boil and pour over the rind. Allow to stand overnight. In the morning, drain syrup and boil several minutes. Pour over rind again. Repeat this step for 3 days.

3. On the third day, cook rind and syrup together for 3 minutes. Pack into jars and seal.

Spiced Cantaloupe

about 2 lbs. cantaloupe
3 cups water
1½ cups vinegar
2¼ cups sugar
1 tsp. salt
1 drop oil of cinnamon
1 drop oil of cloves

1. Peel cantaloupe. Cut into chunks. Pack into jars.
2. Combine remaining ingredients. Bring to a boil. Cool syrup.
3. Pour syrup into packed jars filling to 1" from top of jar. Seal and boil 20 minutes in hot water bath.

"The cantaloupe stay very firm and delicious. I use them for company or just anytime."

Jams
Jellies and Relishes

Zucchini Relish

Makes 3 pints

6 cups zucchini, unpeeled
2 cups onions
1 red pepper
1 green pepper
2½ Tbsp. salt
1¼ cup vinegar
3 cups sugar
2 Tbsp. cornstarch
½ tsp. turmeric
¾ tsp. celery seed
1½ tsp. dry mustard
¼ tsp. nutmeg
¼ tsp. black pepper

1. Grind zucchini, onions, and peppers. Mix vegetables with salt and let stand overnight. Rinse with cold water and drain well.
2. Combine remaining ingredients in a heavy saucepan and cook until slightly thickened. Add vegetable mixture. Cook over low heat for 30 minutes, stirring occasionally. Put into jars and seal.

Variation:
    Substitute cucumbers in place of zucchini.

Cucumber Relish

8 cups cucumbers,   Makes 14 pints
    ground
2 cups onions, ground
¼ cup salt
3 cups sugar
2 cups vinegar
1 tsp. turmeric
1 tsp. celery seed
pinch of alum

1. Mix cucumbers, onions, and salt to-gether. Let stand for 2 hours. Then drain thoroughly.
2. Add remaining ingredients to cucum-ber-onion mixture and simmer for 20 minutes.
3. Pour into jars and seal.

Chow Chow

1 qt. green string beans	Makes about
1 qt. yellow string beans	22 pints
1 qt. celery, chopped	
1 qt. kidney beans	
1 qt. yellow corn	
1 qt. carrots, diced	
1 qt. lima beans	
1 qt. navy beans	
1 qt. cauliflower	
1 qt. small pickles	
12 red peppers, chopped	
3 small onions, minced	
3 lb. sugar	
2 tsp. mustard seed	
2 tsp. celery seed	
2 qt. white vinegar	
1 qt. water	
2 Tbsp. pickling spice	
salt to taste	

1. Cook all vegetables separately until soft but not mushy. Drain and rinse.
2. Make a syrup by combining sugar, mustard seed, celery seed, vinegar, and water. Tie pickling spice in a cloth bag and add to liquid. Bring to a boil.

Remove spice bag and add vegetables. Allow to come to a boil again. Pack chow chow into jars and seal.

French Dressing

½ cup salad oil   Makes 1½ cups
¾ cup sugar
¼ cup vinegar
½ cup ketchup
1 small onion, minced
1½ tsp. paprika
1 tsp. celery seed

Put all ingredients in blender and mix until smooth.

Spaghetti and Pizza Sauce to Can

4 qts. tomatoes, cut in chunks

1. Add water to cover ⅔ tomatoes in stockpot. Cook until soft. Pour into colander to drain off water and juice.
2. Put tomato pulp through a food press to separate seeds and skins from sauce.

Spaghetti Sauce

    2 Tbsp. oil
    2 cloves garlic, minced
    ½ green pepper, chopped
    1 small onion, chopped
    4 cups tomato sauce

1. Sauté first four ingredients together until tender. Then stir in tomato sauce.
2. Pour into jars and boil in water bath for ½ hour.

Pizza Sauce

    1 tsp. Worcestershire sauce
    ¼ tsp. oregano
    ¼ tsp. Italian seasoning

1 ½ tsp. salt
¼ cup sugar
4 cups tomato sauce

1. Simmer all ingredients together for ½ hour.
2. Pour into jars and boil in water bath for ½ hour.

Note:
   You can use the drained juice. If let set, water will separate and can be poured off.

Jams
Jellies and Relishes

Sandwich Spread

4 quarts green tomatoes
1 large red or yellow peppers
1 onions
3 bunches of celery
2 Tbsp. salt
4 cups sugar
4 cups vinegar
1 qt. mayonnaise
6 oz. prepared mustard

1. Cut tomatoes in quarters and remove seeds. Cut peppers in half and remove seeds. Then grind vegetables together, add salt, and let stand overnight.
2. Add sugar and vinegar and boil 25 minutes. Drain off liquid. Chill.
3. When cold, add mayonnaise and mustard. Put in clean jars and store in refrigerator. Spread will keep several months.

Ketchup

2 pecks ripe tomatoes
2 onions
5 stalks celery
2 green peppers
3 cups sugar
2 cups vinegar
¼ tsp. ground cloves
½ tsp. allspice
½ tsp. cinnamon
3 Tbsp. salt

Makes about
6 pints

Cook tomatoes, onions, celery, and peppers until soft and mushy. Pour into colander and drain 8-10 hours. Force remaining pulp through food press or strainer. Place strained mixture in kettle and add remaining ingredients. Boil 10 minutes. Pour into jars and seal.

Jams
Jellies and Relishes

Candies
Beverages and Snacks

from
Amish and Mennonite
kitchens

from
Amish and Mennonite
kitchens

Candies, Beverages and Snacks

Hard workers, lunch box carriers, and children who hike a distance to school or the bus stop find snacks (sweet or salty) and special drinks a happy reward.

Cooks turn out candy, snacks, and pleasing beverages to surprise and celebrate.

Creamy chocolate fudge, peanut goodies, and caramel popcorn were never meant to replace good sturdy meals. Instead, they top them off. Or bring a little relief to a hot afternoon.

Some of these snacks demand a social event. It's no fun making pull taffy or soft pretzels by yourself! And banana crush punch and tomato juice cocktail simply make big batches.

It's time for a break ~ or a party!

Soft Pretzels

2 pkgs. dry yeast
1½ cup warm water
1 tsp. salt
4½ cups flour

Makes 16 large pretzels

Soda Solution

½ cup warm water
2 tsp. soda
salt

1. Dissolve yeast in water. Add salt and flour. Knead until smooth. Cover with a cloth and let rise about 15 minutes.
2. Divide dough into 16 portions. Roll each piece into narrow rolls and shape pretzels. Dip each pretzel in soda solution and sprinkle with salt. Place on greased cookie sheets. Bake at 450° for 15-20 minutes.

Fudge

4 Tbsp. cocoa (or   Makes about 2 lbs.
  3 squares unsweetened baker's chocolate)
3 cups sugar
1 cup milk or cream
3 Tbsp. corn syrup
pinch of salt
2 Tbsp. butter
2 tsp. vanilla

1. Combine cocoa, sugar, milk, syrup, and salt in heavy saucepan. Cook to soft ball stage (236°).
2. Cool slightly and add butter and vanilla. Immediately pour into buttered pan. Allow to harden.

Uncooked Fudge Candy

1 lb. confectioner's Makes about 1¾ lbs.
 sugar
1 cup butter, melted
½ cup crunchy peanut butter
½ cup cocoa
1 tsp. vanilla
pinch of salt

1. Combine all ingredients. Mix well.
2. Spread into greased pan. Cool. Cut into squares.

Easy Creamy Chocolate Fudge

1 lb. real chocolate   Makes about 2 lbs.
1 can condensed milk
pinch of salt
1 tsp. vanilla
½ – 1 cup nuts

1. Melt chocolate in double boiler. Stir in condensed milk. Add salt, vanilla, and nuts.
2. Pour into greased 9" square pan. Cool and cut into squares.

Rocky Road Fudge

1 lb. broken sweet chocolate
2 blocks bitter baking chocolate
2 cups miniature marshmallows
6 oz. chocolate morsels
1 cup pecans, broken

1. Melt sweet and bitter baking chocolate in a double boiler over hot water. Pour half the chocolate into a 9" square baking pan.
2. Pour marshmallows, chocolate morsels, and nuts over the chocolate in the baking pan.
3. Pour remaining melted chocolate over all. Stir slightly until marshmallows and nuts are coated with chocolate.
4. When mixture begins to set, cut into serving pieces. Then refrigerate. Remove pieces from pan only after the candy is cold and hardened.

Peanut Butter Fudge

4 cups sugar
1 cup milk
2 Tbsp. butter
1 Tbsp. vinegar
1 lb. smooth peanut butter
2½ Tbsp. marshmallow whip
1 tsp. vanilla

Makes 1 9"
square pan

1. Mix together in a saucepan the sugar, milk, butter, and vinegar. Boil slowly to the soft ball stage.
2. Remove from heat and stir in peanut butter, marshmallow whip, and vanilla.
3. When mixture begins to set, cut into serving pieces. Then refrigerate. Remove pieces from pan only after the candy is cold and hardened.

Candies
Beverages and Snacks

Mints

¼ cup butter, melted
1 lb. 10x sugar
3 Tbsp. hot water
16 drops or ¼ tsp plus 1 drop
      peppermint
food coloring

1. Mix all ingredients together until smooth and creamy.
2. Shape into small balls and flatten with a fork.

Grandma's Molasses Pull Taffy

3 cups sugar
1 cup molasses
½ cup water
1½ Tbsp butter
2 tsp. flavoring of your choice

1. Butter two 9" cake pans well.
2. Cook sugar, molasses, water, and butter together in a heavy saucepan (to

prevent scorching) to 280° on a candy thermometer, stirring often to prevent sticking. Add flavoring.

3. Pour into prepared cake pans and cool slightly, only until it can be handled. Put on rubber gloves to protect one's hands, find a partner, and begin pulling. (Taffy must be pulled with another person as soon as possible because it hardens quickly!)

4. Pull until taffy becomes very light in color, or white, and forms a rope. Then cut with a kitchen shears into ¾ inch pieces and wrap each in waxed paper.

"Two hints— do this on a clear, cold winter night, and store the finished taffy in a good hiding place so it keeps!"

Candies
Beverages and Snacks

Shellbark Taffy

1½ cups sugar
1 cup water
⅓ cup cider vinegar
3 Tbsp. molasses
½ cup nuts (shellbarks, walnuts, pecans, or peanuts)

1. Combine sugar, water, vinegar, and molasses. Bring to a boil and boil to a hard~crack stage (taffy turns hard when dropped into cold water).
2. Spread nuts in the bottom of a buttered 9" square pan. Pour taffy over nuts. Cool at room temperature. Before completely cold, mark squares with a knife. When cold, break apart on markings.

Best Ever Caramels

2 cups sugar　　　　Makes about 3½ lbs.
1 cup brown sugar
1 cup light corn syrup
1 cup heavy cream
1 cup milk
1 cup butter
1¼ tsp. vanilla

1. Combine sugars, syrup, cream, milk, and butter. Mix well. Cook slowly, stirring occasionally until mixture reaches firm ball stage (248°). Remove from heat. Add vanilla.
2. Pour into greased 8"x 8"x 2" pan. Cool. When firm, turn onto a board and cut caramels with heavy knife or shears. Wrap each square in waxed paper.

Variations:
1. Substitute 2 cups half and half in place of heavy cream and milk.
2. Coat completed caramels with chocolate.
3. Add ½ cup chopped pecans with vanilla.

Candies
Beverages and Snacks

Date and Nut Balls

1 cup dates, chopped   Makes 30-40 balls
½ cup butter or margarine
2 eggs
1 cup sugar
2 cups rice krispies cereal
½ cup nuts, chopped
coconut, finely shredded

1. Mix dates, butter, eggs, and sugar together in a saucepan. Cook 10 minutes, stirring constantly.
2. Cool, then add cereal and nuts.
3. Form mixture into balls and roll in coconut.

Honey Milk Balls

1 cup oatmeal   Makes about 2½ dozen
1 cup powdered milk
½ cup honey
½ cup crunchy peanut butter

Combine all ingredients. Mix well. Form 1" balls.

Caramel Popcorn

3¾ quarts popped popcorn
1 cup brown sugar
½ cup margarine
¼ cup light corn syrup
½ tsp. salt
½ tsp. baking soda
½ tsp. vanilla

1. Pour popped popcorn into a large roasting pan.
2. Mix sugar, margarine, corn syrup, and salt in a saucepan and cook gently over medium heat, stirring constantly. When the mixture begins to boil, cook for 5 more minutes.
3. Remove syrup from heat and stir in soda and vanilla until the mixture becomes foamy. Pour syrup over popcorn, stirring to coat.
4. Bake for 1 hour at 200°, stirring every 15 minutes. Then cool and crumble into small pieces.

Candies
Beverages and Snacks

Peanut Goodies

Graham crackers
½ cup margarine, melted
1 cup brown sugar
chopped peanuts

1. Line a cookie sheet with a single layer of graham crackers.
2. Combine margarine and sugar. Spread over crackers. Sprinkle with peanuts. Bake at 350° for 10 minutes.

Peanut Butter Bon-Bons

2 cups peanut butter   Makes about 6 dozen
½ cup butter
1 lb. confectioner's sugar
3 cups Rice Krispies cereal
chocolate for coating

1. Combine all ingredients except the chocolate. Mix well. Roll into 1" balls. Chill.
2. Dip in melted chocolate.

Hello Dollies

Makes 25 squares

¼ cup butter or margarine, melted
1 cup graham cracker crumbs
1 cup coconut, shredded
1 cup chocolate bits
1 cup pecans, chopped
1 can sweetened, condensed milk

1. Spread melted butter on bottom of a 9" square pan.
2. Add a layer of graham cracker crumbs; then a layer of coconut, a layer of chocolate bits, and a layer of pecans. Pour condensed milk over all.
3. Bake at 325° for 30 minutes. Cool and cut into squares.

Candies
Beverages and Snacks

Sesame Crunch

Makes about 2 lbs.

2 cups sugar
1 cup honey
1 tsp. butter
½ cup water
2½ cups sesame seeds
1 tsp. baking soda
1 tsp. vanilla

1. In heavy saucepan, combine sugar, honey, butter, and water. Cook to 290° being careful not to scorch the mixture.
2. Remove from heat and add remaining ingredients. Pour into a well greased shallow pan (10"x 15"x 1"). When partially cooled mark cutting lines. When cold, crack apart on indentations.

Kisses

Makes about 5 dozen

3 egg whites
2 cups + 1 Tbsp. sugar
2 tsp. vinegar
1 tsp. vanilla
2 cups flaked coconut

1. Beat egg whites till frothy. Gradually add sugar and vinegar. Beat until fluffy (about 10 minutes). Stir in vanilla and coconut.
2. Drop by teaspoons onto cookie sheets. Bake at 250° for 30~45 minutes.

Variation:
Crushed nuts may be substituted for coconut.

Rhubarb Punch
2 lb. tender rhubarb
5 cups water
¼ cup lemon juice
sugar
grapefruit juice
1 qt. ginger-ale

Chop rhubarb. Combine rhubarb with water and cook to a mush. Strain well, reserving only the juice. Add lemon juice. For each cup juice add ⅓ cup sugar and ½ cup grapefruit juice. Chill well. Just before serving, add chilled ginger-ale.

from
Amish and Mennonite
kitchens

Nutritious Fruit Punch

1 large can   Makes 2 gallons
   pineapple juice
1 12 oz. can frozen orange
   juice concentrate
1 quart peaches
1 banana
3 lemons
1 cup sugar, optional

1. Combine pineapple and orange juices in a large container.
2. Mix peaches and banana in blender and puree. Add to juices.
3. Grate rind of 1 lemon. Then juice all 3 lemons. Stir rind and lemon juice into juice mixture.
4. Add sugar, if desired. Add enough water to make 2 gallons. Chill and serve.

Cranberry Punch

1 lb. cranberries   Makes about 1½ gals
7 cups water
2½ cups sugar

2 bottles ginger-ale
2 cups frozen orange juice concentrate
juice of one lemon
2 qts. water

Boil cranberries in 4 cups of water. Drain juice. Combine sugar with remaining water and boil 5 minutes. Combine with cranberry juice. Add all other ingredients. Serve well chilled.

Sparkling Punch

1 6 oz. can frozen lemonade

Makes about 5 qts.

1 6 oz. can frozen Hawaiian Punch
2 6 oz. cans frozen orange juice
2 qts. water
2 qts. ginger-ale or 7-up

Combine all ingredients and mix well. Serve well chilled.

Banana Crush Punch

4 cups sugar
6 cups water
1 large can pineapple juice
5 bananas, crushed
juice of 5 oranges
juice of 2 lemons
ginger-ale or 7-up

1. Combine sugar and water. Boil for 1 minute. Cool.
2. Mix juices and bananas. Add syrup and mix well. Freeze in ice cube trays or pint containers. When ready to serve, place ice cubes in glass and fill with ginger-ale or place 1 pint in a 2 qt. pitcher and fill with ginger-ale. Allow punch concentrate to melt so flavors can blend with ginger-ale before serving.

Orange Julius

1 6 oz. can   Makes about 1 qt.
    frozen orange juice
1 cup milk
1 cup water

¼ cup sugar
2 tsp. vanilla
5~6 ice cubes

Combine all ingredients in blender and mix well.

Lemonade

4 lemons   Makes 1 gallon
3 cups sugar
1 quart hot water
3 quarts cold water

1. Wash and slice lemons. Remove seeds. Stomp lemon slices and sugar together with a potato masher until well mixed.
2. Add hot water to lemon and sugar mixture and stir to dissolve sugar and extract the lemon pulp and juice.
3. Squeeze lemon slices by hand to get balance of juice before disposing of slices. Add cold water to mixture and stir until well blended. Chill and serve.

Candies
Beverages and Snacks

Grape Juice

10 lbs. grapes
2 cups water
1½ lb. sugar

1. Wash grapes, add water, and cook until soft. Drain through fruit press until juice stops flowing.
2. Add sugar and stir until dissolved.
3. Bring juice to a boil, then pour into jars or bottles and seal.
4. To serve, mix grape juice concentrate with an equal amount of water.

Variation:
Stir in frozen lemonade concentrate to taste just before serving.

Tomato Juice Cocktail

12 quarts tomatoes, cut in chunks
2 medium green peppers, chopped
2 small celery stalks, chopped fine
1 medium onion, chopped fine
2⅔ cups sugar

Makes about 14 quarts

¼ cup salt
1 tsp. black pepper

1. Put all raw vegetables together in a large stockpot. Add water to a depth of 1 inch. Cook slowly until tender, then put through food press.
2. Pour pureed mixture back into the stockpot and stir in the seasonings. Bring to a boil.
3. Pour into canning jars and seal.

Hot Punch

2 cups strong   Makes about 1 gal.
    tea (2 cups water to 8 tea bags)
2½ cups sugar
2 qts. water
5 cups orange juice
1 cup lemon juice

Dissolve 1½ cups sugar in tea. Combine remaining sugar and water. Bring to a boil. Add all other ingredients. Serve piping hot.

Mint Meadow Tea

1 cup sugar   Makes ½ gallon
1 pint water
1 cup fresh tea leaves, either peppermint
      or spearmint
juice of 1 lemon
water

1. Stir sugar and pint of water together in a saucepan and bring to a boil.
2. Pour boiling syrup over tea leaves and let steep for 20 minutes. Remove the leaves and let tea cool.
3. Add the lemon juice and enough water to make ½ gallon of tea.
4. Serve either hot or cold.

Peppermint Drink

2 qts. ice water
½ cup sugar
a few drops Essence of Peppermint or
      Peppermint Spirits

Combine all ingredients and mix well. Serve ice cold.

24~Hour Root Beer

1 tsp. dry yeast   Makes 1 gallon
1 cup lukewarm water
2 cups sugar
5 tsp. root beer extract
lukewarm water
6~10 dried raisins

1. Dissolve yeast in 1 cup lukewarm water. Let stand 5 minutes.
2. Combine sugar and extract. Add yeast mixture to it. Pour into gallon jug, then fill with lukewarm water, stopping 1 inch from the top. Add dried raisins for flavor.
3. Cover jar and set in the sun for 3 hours. Refrigerate overnight. Drink the next day!

Candies
Beverages and Snacks

Hot Chocolate

Makes 1 qt.

4 rounded tsp.
    cocoa powder
8 tsp. sugar
pinch of salt
¾ cup hot water
3¼ cups milk
1 tsp. vanilla

1. Mix cocoa, sugar, salt, and water together in a pan. Bring to a boil, then stir. Repeat two more times, watching carefully that the mixture doesn't scorch.
2. Add milk and vanilla and heat thoroughly.

Variation:
    Add a dollop of whipped cream or marshmallow on top of each cup before serving.

Cheese Ball

3 3 oz. packages cream   Makes 1 ball
    cheese, or 1 6 oz. pack and 1 3oz. pack
1 3 oz. package chive cream cheese
¼ lb. blue cheese or Roquefort cheese,
    crumbled
1 small onion, grated
1 Tbsp. horseradish
chopped pecans
parsley flakes

1. Allow cheeses to reach room temperature. Then mix the cheeses, onion, and horseradish until thoroughly combined. Store in the refrigerator until firm, at least 1 hour.
2. Form mixture into a ball. Mix chopped pecans and parsley flakes together. Then roll cheese ball in the nuts and parsley, turning it over and over until fully covered.
3. Wrap in foil and refrigerate until ready to serve.

from
Amish and Mennonite kitchens

Pineapple-Pecan Cheese Ball

2 8 oz. packages   Makes 2 balls
    cream cheese
1 18½ oz. can crushed pineapple, drained
2 cups pecans, chopped
¼ cup green pepper, chopped
2 Tbsp. onion, chopped fine
1 Tbsp. salt

1. Allow cream cheese to reach room temperature. Then mix all ingredients thoroughly.
2. Chill until firm, at least 1 hour. Then form into 2 balls, wrapping each in tin foil and refrigerating until ready to serve.

"O-o-o, we like it!"

Easter Cheese

2 qt. milk
4 eggs
2 cups buttermilk or sour milk
1 tsp. salt
½ tsp. sugar

1. Heat sweet milk to boiling point.
2. Beat eggs lightly. Add buttermilk, salt, and sugar. Beat lightly again. Pour slowly into hot milk.
3. Cover milk and allow to stand for several minutes. Stir slowly until mixture separates. Remove cheese from whey with a large slotted spoon or collander. Place cheese in mold and chill until set.

"This is a delicious spread on bread along with honey or molasses!"

Candies
Beverages and Snacks

from
Amish and Mennonite
kitchens

Scramble

2 lbs. mixed nuts or   Makes 8 qts.
    peanuts
1   12 oz. package Wheat Chex
1   10 oz. package Cheerios
1   6½ oz. package Rice Chex
1   6½ oz. package pretzel sticks
1   6½ oz. package pretzel nuggets
2 cups salad oil
2 Tbsp. Worcestershire sauce
1 Tbsp. garlic salt
1 Tbsp. seasoned salt

1. Combine all ingredients in very large roaster. Mix well.
2. Bake at 250° for 2 hours, stirring every 15 minutes. Store in tight container.

"This is a good snack for a big crowd, especially young people!"

Index

Index

Index

Index

Index

Index

Index

Index

Index

Index

Index

Index

412

Index

from
Amish and Mennonite kitchens

About the Authors

Phyllis Pellman Good is editor of <u>Festival Quarterly</u>, a magazine exploring the art, faith, and culture of Mennonite peoples. She and her husband Merle oversee The People's Place and the Old Country Store. Phyllis is the author of several books, among them <u>Cooking and Memories</u>.

The Goods are the parents of two daughters and are members of the Landisville Mennonite Church.

Rachel Thomas Pellman is manager of the Old Country Store in Intercourse, Pa., which features quilts, crafts, and toys by more than two hundred Amish and Mennonite craftspersons. Rachel and her husband Kenny are co-authors of <u>The World of Amish Quilts</u> and its companion book, <u>Amish Quilt Patterns</u>.

Rachel and Kenny are the parents of one son and are members of the Rossmere Mennonite Church.

Phyllis and Rachel are sisters-in-law.

<u>From Amish and Mennonite Kitchens</u> is on sale in many bookstores and shops across North America. It is also available from its publisher. Request a special order form from Good Books, Intercourse, Pennsylvania, 17534.

Notes

from
Amish and Mennonite
kitchens

Now You Can Own Any or All of the
AMISH SEASONS PANORAMA PRINTS

Collect these beautiful prints!
Individually hand-signed by the artist.

Summer

Winter

Seedtime

Harvest

Please send me the following:

_____ copies of **Summer** (10″ x 20″) @ $20.00 ea. _____

_____ copies of **Winter** (10″ x 20″) @ $20.00 ea. _____

_____ copies of **Seedtime** (10″ x 20″) @ $20.00 ea. _____

_____ copies of **Harvest** (10″ x 20″) @ $20.00 ea. _____

_____ copies of **Summer** (6″ x 12″) @ $10.00 ea. _____

_____ copies of **Winter** (6″ x 12″) @ $10.00 ea. _____

_____ copies of **Seedtime** (6″ x 12″) @ $10.00 ea. _____

_____ copies of **Harvest** (6″ x 12″) @ $10.00 ea. _____

Subtotal $ _____

PA Residents add 6% sales tax $ _____

Shipping and Handling $ _____
(Add 10%, $3.50 minimum)

For UPS add $1.00 additional $ _____

GRAND TOTAL $ _____

Name _____

Address _____

City _____ State/Province _____ Zip _____

Phone number _____

Mail with payment in U.S. funds to: **Good Books,
PO Box 419, Intercourse, PA 17534.**

*If you don't want to cut your beautiful cookbook, simply make a
copy of this page so you can order. Or call 800/762-7171 to order
by credit card.*